DE TURKEY AND DE LAW

DE TURKEY AND DE LAW

Zora Neale Hurston

www.General-Books.net

Publication Data:

Title: De Turkey and De Law
Author: Hurston, Zora Neale, 1901?-1960
Reprinted: 2010, General Books, Memphis, Tennessee, USA

How We Made This Book for You
We made this book exclusively for you using patented Print on Demand technology.
First we scanned the original rare book using a robot which automatically flipped and photographed each page.
We automated the typing, proof reading and design of this book using Optical Character Recognition (OCR) software on the scanned copy. That let us keep your cost as low as possible.
If a book is very old, worn and the type is faded, this can result in numerous typos or missing text. This is also why our books don't have illustrations; the OCR software can't distinguish between an illustration and a smudge.
We understand how annoying typos, missing text or illustrations, foot notes in the text or an index that doesn't work, can be. That's why we provide a free digital copy of most books exactly as they were originally published. You can also use this PDF edition to read the book on the go. Simply go to our website (www.general-books.net) to check availability. And we provide a free trial membership in our book club so you can get free copies of other editions or related books.
OCR is not a perfect solution but we feel it's more important to make books available for a low price than not at all. So we warn readers on our website and in the descriptions we provide to book sellers that our books don't have illustrations and may have numerous typos or missing text. We also provide excerpts from books to book sellers and on our website so you can preview the quality of the book before buying it.
If you would prefer that we manually type, proof read and design your book so that it's perfect, simply contact us for the cost. Since many of our books only sell one or two copies a year, unlike mass market books we have to split the production costs between those one or two buyers.

Limit of Liability/Disclaimer of Warranty:
The publisher and author make no representations or warranties with respect to the accuracy or completeness of the book. The advice and strategies in the book may not be suitable for your situation. You should consult with a professional where appropriate. The publisher is not liable for any damages resulting from the book.
Please keep in mind that the book was written long ago; the information is not current. Furthermore, there may be typos, missing text or illustration and explained above.

1

DE TURKEY AND DE LAW

DE TURKEY AND DE LAW
A COMEDY IN THREE ACTS
by
   ZORA HURSTON
CAST
Jim Weston A young man and the town bully (A Methodist)
   Dave Carter The town's best hunter and fisherman (Baptist)
   Joe Clarke The Mayor, Postmaster, storekeeper
   Daisy Blunt The town vamp
   Lum Boger The Marshall
   Walter Thomas A villager (Methodist)
   Lige Moseley A villager (Methodist)
   Joe Lindsay A villager (Baptist)
   Della Lewis A villager (Baptist)
   Tod Hambo A villager (Baptist)
   Lucy Taylor A villager (Methodist)
   Rev. Singletary (Baptist)
   Rev. Simms (Methodist)

Villagers, children, dogs.

ACT I

SETTING: A Negro village in Florida in our own time. All action from viewpoint of an actor facing audience.

PLACE: Joe Clarke's store porch in the village. A frame building with a false front. A low porch with two steps up. Door in center of porch. A window on each side of the door. A bench on each side of the porch. Axhandles, hoes and shovels, etc. are displayed leaning against the wall. Exits right and left. Street is unpaved. Grass and weeds growing all over.

TIME: It is late afternoon on a Saturday in summer.

Before the curtain rises the voices of children are heard, boisterous at play. Shouts and laughter.

VOICE OF ONE BOY Naw, I don't want to play wringing no dish rag! We gointer play chick mah chick mah craney crow.

GIRL'S VOICE
Yeah, less play dat, and I'm gointer to be de hen.

BOY'S VOICE And I'm gointer be de hawk. Lemme git myself a stick to mark wid. (The curtain rises slowly. As it goes up the game is being organized. The boy who is the hawk is squatting center stage in the street before the store with a short twig in his hand. The largest girl is lining up the other children behind her.)

THE MOTHER HEN (looking back over her flock) Y'all ketch holt of one 'nother's clothes so de hauk can't git yuh. (They do.) Y'all straight now?

CHORUS
Yeah. (The march around the hawk commences.)

HEN AND CHICKS
Chick mah chick mah craney crow
Went to de well to wash my toe
When I come back my chick was gone.
What time ole witch?

HAWK (making a tally on the ground) One!

HEN AND CHICKS Chick mah chick etc.–(While this is going on Walter Thomas from the store door eating peanuts from a bag appears and seats himself on the porch beside the steps.)

HAWK
(Scoring again) Two!
(Enter a little girl right. She trots up to
the big girl.)

LITTLE GIRL (officiously) Titter, mama say if you don't come on wid dat soap she gointer wear you out.

HEN AND CHICKS Chick mah chick etc. (While this is being sung, enter Joe Lindsay and seats himself on right bench. He lights his pipe. The little girl stands b by the fence rubbing her leg with her foot.

HAWK (scoring) Three!

LITTLE GIRL (insistent) Titter, titter! Mama say to tell you to come on home wid dat soap and rake up dat yard. I bet she gointer beat you good.

BIG GIRL (angrily) Aw naw, mama ain't sent you after me, nothin' of de kind! Gwan home and leave me alone.

LITTLE GIRL You better come on! I'm gointer tell mama how 'omanish you actin cause you in front of dese boys.

BIG GIRL (makes a threatenin' gesture) Aw don't be so fast and showin' off in company. Ack lak you ain't got no sense!

LITTLE GIRL (starts to cry) Dat's all right. I'm going home and tell mama you down here playing wid boys and she sho gointer whup you good, too. I'm gointer tell her you called me a fool too, now. (She walks off, wiping her eyes and nose with the back of her hand) Yeah, I'm goin' tell her! Jus' showin' off in front of ole John Wesley Taylor. I'm going to tell her too, now.

BIG GIRL (flounces her skirt) Tell her! Tell her! Turn her up and smell her! (Game resumed) Chick mah chick etc.

HAWK Four! (He arises and imitates a hawk flying and trying to catch a chicken. Calling in a high voice.) Chickie!!

HEN
(Flapping her wings to protect her young) My chickens' sleep.

HAWK
Chickie!!

HEN
My chickens' sleep.

HAWK
I shall have a chick.

HEN
You shan't have a chick.

HAWK
I'm going home. (flies off)

HEN
There's de road.

HAWK
I'm comin' back.

(During this dialog the hawk is feinting and darting in his efforts to catch a chicken and the chickens are dancing defensively.)

HEN
Don't keer if you do.

HAWK
My pot's a boiling.

HEN
Let it boil.

HAWK
My guts a growling

HEN
Let 'em growl.

HAWK
I must have a chick.

HEN
You shan't have nairn.
HAWK
My mama's sick.
HEN
Let her die.
HAWK
Chickie!!
HEN
My chicken's sleep.
(Hawk darts quickly around the hen and grabs a chicken and leads him off and places the captive on his knees at the store porch. After a brief bit of dancing he catches another, then a third who is a chubby little boy. The little boy begins to cry.)
LITTLE BOY
I ain't gointer play cause you hurt me.
HAWK
Aw, naw, I din't hurt you.
LITTLE BOY Yeah you did too. You pecked me right here. (points to top of his head)
HAWK Well if you so touchous you got to cry every time anybody look at you, you can't play wid us.
LITTLE BOY (smothering sobs) I ain't cryin'. (He is placed with the other captives. Hawk returns to game.)
HAWK
Chickie.
HEN
My chickens sleep!
VOICE FROM A DISTANCE
Titter! You Titter!!!
BIG GIRL
Yessum
VOICE
If you don't come here wid dat soap you better!
BIG GIRL (shakes herself poutingly, half sobs) Soon's I git grown I'm gointer run away. Everytime a person gits to havin' fun, it's "come here, Titter and rake de yard." She don't never make Bubber do nothin. (She exits into the store.)
HAWK
Now we ain't got no hen.
ALL THE GIRLS (in a clamor) I'll be de mama hen! Lemme be it! (Enter Hambo left and stands looking at the children.)
HAMBO
Can't dese young uns keep up a powerful racket, Joe?
LINDSAY They sho kin. They kin git round so vi'grous when they whoopin and hollerin and rompin and racin, but just put 'em to work now and you kin count dead lice fallin' off of 'em.

(Enter Tillie from the store with the soap. Hambo pulls out a plug of tobacco from his hip pocket and bites a chunk from it.)

HAMBO

De way dese chillun is dese days is,–eat? Yes! Squall and holler? Yes! Kick out shoes? Yes! Work? No!!

LINDSAY You sho is tellin' de truth. Now look at dese! I'll bet everyone of 'em's mammies sent 'em to de store an' they out here frollickin'. If one of 'em was mine, I'd whup 'em till they couldn't set down. (to the children) Shet up dat racket and gwan home! (The children pay no attention and the game gets hotter.)

DISTANT VOICE (off stage) You Tit-ter!! You Tit-Ter!!

WALTER

Titter, don't you hear yo' ma callin' you?

ESSIE

Yessuh, I mean naw suh.

LINDSAY How come you can't answer, then? Lawd knows de folks just ruins chilluns dese days. Deys skeered tuh whup 'em right. Den before they gits twenty de gals done come up wid somethin' in dey arms an' de boys on de chain gang. If you don't whup 'em, they'll whip you.

HAMBO Dat sho is whut de Lawd loves. When I wuz a boy they *raised* chillen then. Now they lets 'em do as they please. There ain't no real chestizing no more. They takes a lil tee-ninchy switch and tickles em. No wonder de world is in sich uh mess.

VOICE OFF STAGE

You Tit-ter!! Aw Titter!!

ESSIE (stops to listen) Yessum!!

VOICE OFF STAGE

If you don't come here, you better!

ESSIE Yessum! (to her playmates) Aw shucks! I got to go home. (She exits right, walking sullenly. The game has stopped.)

LINDSAY (pointing at Essie) You see dat gal shakin' herself at her mammy? De sassy lil binch needs her guts stomped out. (to Essie) Run! I'm comin' on down there an' tell yo' ma how 'omanish you is, shakin' yo'self at grown folks. (Essie walks slower and shakes her skirt contemptously. Lindsay jumps to his feet as if to pursue her.) You must smell yo'self! (Essie exits.) Now de rest of you haitians scatter way from in front dis store. Dis ain't no place for chillen, nohow. (gesture of shooing) Gwan! Thin out! Every time a grownperson open they mouf y'all right dere to gaze down they throat. Git! (The children exit sullenly right. In the silence that follows the cracking of Walter's peanut shells can be heard very plainly.)

HAMBO Walter, God a' mighty! You better quit eatin' 'em ground peas de way you do. You gointer die wid de colic.

LINDSAY Aw, taint gointer hurt him. I don't b'lieve uh cord uh wood would lay heavy on Walter's belly. He kin eat mo' penders than Brazzle's mule.

WALTER (laughing) Aw naw, don't throw me in wid dat mule. He could eat up camp-meetin, back off scociation and drink Jurdan dry.

LINDSAY
And still stay so po' till he wuzn't nothin atall but a mule frame.
(Enter Lige Moseley right) Taint never been no mule in de world lak
dat ole yaller mule since Jonah went to joppy.

(Lige seats himself on the floor on the other side of the steps. Pulls out a bone toothpick and begins to pick his teeth)

LIGE
Y'all still talkin bout Brazzle's ole useter-be mule?

HAMBO
Yeah. Memeber dat time Brazzle hitched him to de plow and took him to
Eshleman's new ground?

LIGE And he laid down before he'd plow a lick. Sho I do! But who ever seen him work? All you ever did see was him and Brazzle fightin up and down de furrows. (all laugh) He was so mean he would even try to kick you if you went in his stall to carry him some corn.

WALTER Nothin but pure concentrated meanness stuffed into uh mule hide. Thass de reason he wouldn't git fat–just too mean.

LIGE Sho was skinny now. You could use his ribs for a washboard and hang de clothes up on his hips to dry. (all laugh)

HAMBO Lige, you kin lie [Note: "like" crossed out] lak cross ties [Note inserted text: from Jacksonville to Key West.]. But layin all sides to jokes, when they told me dat mule was dead, uh just took and knocked off from work to see him drug out lak all de rest of de folks, and folkses dat mule wuz too contrary to lay down on his side and die. He laid on his raw-boney back wid his foots stickin straight up in de air lak he wuz fightin something.

LINDSAY He wuz–bet he fought ole death lak a natural man. Ah seen his bones yistiddy, out dere on de edge of de cypress swamp. De buzzards done picked em clean and de elements done bleached em.

LIGE Everybody went to dat draggin out. Even Joe Clarke shet up his store dat mornin and went (turns his head and calls into the store) didn't you, Mr. Clarke?

CLARKE'S VOICE
Didn't I whut? (enters and stands in door)

LIGE
Shet up yo' store and go to de draggin out of Brazzle's ole mule.

CLARKE I, God, Yeah. It was worth it. (sees Hambo) I didn't know you was out here. Lemme beat you uh game of checkers.

HAMBO Lissen at de ole tush hawg! Well, go git de board, and lemme beat you a pair of games befo' de mail gits in.

CLARKE (to the others) Beat old me! (to Hambo) Come on here, youse my fish. (calls into store) Mattie bring me dat checker-board and de checkers! (to men on porch) You got to talk to wimmen-folks lak dat–tell 'em every lil' thing–do she'd come rackin out here wid de board by itself.

(Enter Mrs. Clarke with homemade checker-board and coffee can containing the much-used checkers. Clarke sits on a keg and faces Hambo. They put the board on their knees and pour out the checkers)

HAMBO
You want black or red?

CLARKE Oh, I don't keer which–I'm gointer beat you anyhow. You take de black. (they arrange them. The others get near to look on. Hambo sits looking at the board without moving.)

HAMBO
Who's first move?

CLARKE Black folks always go to work first. Move! (Hambo moves and the same proceeds with the spectators very interested. Enter Lum Boger [Note: Handwritten correction: Bailey] right and joins the spectators. A woman enters left with a market basket and goes on in the store. The checkers click on the board. A girl about twelve enters right and goes into the store and comes out with a stick of peppermint candy.

WALTER Naw you don't Hambo!–Don't you go in dere! Dats a trap–(pointing) come right here and you got him.

LIGE
Back dat man up (pointing) Hambo do he'll git et up.
(there is the noise of the checkers for a half minute then a general shout of triumph)

SPECTATORS
You got him now, Hambo! Clarke, he's sho got you.

CLARKE
(Chagrined) Aw, he aint done nothin! Jes' watch ME.

HAMBO
(Jeering) Yeah, gwan move! Ha! Ha! go head and move.

SPECTATORS
Aw, he got you, Bro. Mayor–might as well give up. He got you in de
Louisville loop.

CLARKE Give up what? He can't beat me? (peeved) de rest of y'all git from over me, whoopin and hollerin! I God, a man can't hear his ears.
(The men fall back revealing the players clearly)

HAMBO Aw, neb mind bout them, Joe, go head and move. You aint got but one move to make nohow–go head on and take it.

CLARKE (moving a checker) Aw, here.

HAMBO (triumphant) Now! watch me boys whut Ahm gonna do to him. Ahm gonna laff in notes, while Ah work on him. (he lifts a checker high in the air preparatory to the jump, laughing to the scale and counting each checker he jumps out loud) Do, sol, fa, me, la! One! (jumps a checker) la, sol, fa, me, do! Two! (jumps another) Do, re, fa, me, do, Three! Me, re, la, so, fa! Four! (the crowd is roaring with laughter) Sol, fa, me, la, sol, do! Five! Ha! Ha! boys I got [Note: "the" x-ed out] de ole tush hawg! I got him in de go-long. (He slaps his leg and accidently knocks the board off his knee and spills the checkers.)

CLARKE Too bad you done dat, Hambo, cause Ah was gointer beat you at dat (he rises and starts towards the door of the store as the crowd roars in laughter)

HAMBO
You mean you was gointer beat me to de door, not a game Of checkers.
Ah done run de ole coon in his hole.

LIGE Well, Hambo, you done got to be so hard at checkers, come on less see whut you can do wid de cards. (He pulls out a soiled deck from his coat pocket and moves toward the bench at the left of the porch) You take Lum and me and Walter will wear you out.

HAMBO
You know I don't play no cards.

LUM
We aint playin for no money, just a lil Florida flip.

HAMBO Y'all can't play no Florida flip. 'Fore Ah joined de church there wasn't a man in de state could beat me wid de cards. But Ahm a deacon now, in Macedonia Baptist–Ah don't bother wid de cards no mo". (He and Joe Lindsay go inside store)

LIGE
Well, come on Lum. Walter, git yo'self a partner.

WALTER
(Looking about) Taint nobody to git (looks off right) Here come Dave
Carter.

LIGE You can't do nothin wid him dese days. He useter choose a game of cards when he wasn't out huntin, but now when he ain't out huntin varmints he's huntin' Daisy Blunt. (Enter Dave right with a shot-gun slung over his shoulder.)

WALTER Come on, fish, lemme bend a five-up over yo' head. You looks just like my meat.

DAVE Ahm on mah way to kill me a turkey gobbler, but if you and Lum thinks y'all's tush hawgs Ah'll stop long enough to take you down a button-hole lower. (He sets his gun down and finds a seat and draws it up to the card table)

WALTER Naw, Dave, we aint going to fool wid no button-holes we gointer tear off de whole piece dat de button-holes is in. (They all get set) All right boys, turn it on and let de bad luck happen.

LIGE
(Probbing the deck) My deal.

WALTER Watch yo'self Dave, don't get to worryin bout Daisy and let 'em ketch yo' jack.

LUM
(Winking) What you reckon he gointer be worryin' bout Daisy for? Dot's
Jim's gal.

DAVE Air Lawd, a heap sees but a few knows. Deal de cards man–you shufflin' a mighty lot.

WALTER
Sho is–must be tryin' to carry de cut to us.

LIGE Aw, we ain't gonna cheat you, we gonna beat you. (He slams down the cards for Dave to cut) Wanna cut 'em?

DAVE
Nope. Taint no use cuttin' a rabbit out when you kin twist him out.
Deal 'em! (Lige deals and turns up Jack of spades.)

WALTER
Yee-ee! Did you snatch dat Jack?

LIGE

Man, you know I ain't snatched no Jack. Whut you doin'?

WALTER

I'm beggin!

LIGE

Go ahead and tell 'em I sent you.

WALTER Play just like ahm in New York, partner. (scratches his head) We oughter try to ketch dat Jack.

LIGE

Stick out yo' hand an' you'll draw back a nub.

WALTER

Whut you want me to play for you, partner?

DAVE

Play me a baby diamond.

(Walter plays, then Lum, then Dave)

LUM (Triumphant) Looka pardner, they doin all dat woofin on uh queen–sendin' women to do uh man's work. Watch me stomp her wid mah king (He slams his card down and collects the trick.) Now come un under dis ace! (They all play and he collects the trick.) Now whut you want me to play for you, pardner?

LIGE

How many times you seen de deck.

LUM

Twice

LIGE

Pull off wid yo' king.

(Lum plays the king of spades. All the others play.) Look at ole low pardner. Ah knowed ah wuz gointer ketch him! Come right back at 'em.

LUM (stands up and slams down the ace) Pack up, pardner. Ahm playin' mah knots, now all play now. Ho! Ho! Dere goes de queen'. De Jack's a gentleman! (Lige takes the Jack and sticks it up on his forehead in braggadocia.) Here comes de ten spot, pardner, ahm dumpin to yuh!

LIGE (as he plays the Jack) Everybody git up off it and dump. High, low, Jack, game and gone from de first four.

WALTER

Gimme dem cards! Y'all carried de cub to us dat time. (riffles the cards elaborately) but de deal is in de high, tall house now. Dis is Booker T Washington spreadin his mess. (offers cards to Lige) Cut?

LIGE

Yeah, cut 'em and shoot 'em. I'd cut behind mah ma. (He cuts and Walter deals.)

WALTER

Well, whut sayin'?

LUM

I'm beggin.

WALTER

Get up off yo' knees. Youse dat one.

LIGE

Walter, you sho stacked dese cards.

WALTER Aw, stop cryin' and play, man. Youse too old to be hollerin' titty-mama.

LUM Dis ain't no hand, dis is a foot. What you want me to play for you partner?

LIGE Play yo' own hand partner–I ain't nobody. Lead yo' bosses. (He leads the ace of clubs. Play goes round to dealer and Walter takes the card off the deck and slams it down.)

WALTER Get up ol' deuce of diamonds and gallop off wid yo' load. Pardner, how many times you seen de deck?

DAVE

(Two times–(they make signals.)

WALTER Watch dis ol' queen. Less go! (He begins to sing–Dave joins in.) When yo' card gits lucky, oh pardner, you oughter be in a rollin' game. (He speaks.) Ha! Ha! Wash day and no soap! (He sticks the Jack upon his forehead. He stands up and sings again.) Ahm goin' to de 'Bama Lawd. Pardner don't want no change. (He collects that trick and plays again. Dave also stands.)

DAVE Here come de man from de White House–ol' king of diamonds. (Sings, all join.) Ahm goin' back to de Bama, Lawd. Pardner won't be worried wid you. (He collects the trick.) Never had no trouble, Lour pardner, till I stopped by here.

(They all stand hilariously slam down their cards.

WALTER Aw, wese just too hard for you boys–we eats our dinner out de blacksmith shop. Y'all can't bully dis game. (He solemnly reaches over and takes Dave's hand.)

DAVE (to Walter) Mr. Hoover, you sho is a noble president. We done stuck dese shad-moufs full of cobs. They skeered to play us any mo'.

LIGE Who skeered? Y'all jus' playin ketch up nohow. Git back down and lemme wrap uh five-up round yo' neck.

DAVE (looking off right) Squat dat rabbit an' less jump another one. Here come Daisy.

WALTER Aw Lord, you ain't no mo' good now. But Ah don't blame you, Dave, she looks warm.

(Enter Daisy right with a scarlet hibiscus over each ear and smiling broadly.)

LIGE (jumps down and takes Daisy by the arm) Come on up here, Daisy and ease Dave's pain. He's so crazy 'bout you his heart 'bout to burn a hole in his shirt. (She steps up on the porch)

DAVE

(Bashfully) Aw, y'all gwan. Ah kin talk.

DAISY

(Arms akimbo, impudently) Oh kin you? (She gets up close to Dave)

DAVE

(Pleased) You better git way from me fore Jim come long.

DAISY (Coquettishly) Ain't you man enough to cover de ground you stand on?

DAVE

Oh, Ah can back my crap! Don't worry 'bout me. Where you headed for?

DAISY

Where *you* goin? (Audaciously)

DAVE Out by de cypress swamp to kill us uh turkey. Its uh great big ole gobbler–been slurring me fer six months. Ahm gointer git him today for you, and yo' mama gointer cook him.

DAISY

Ah sho would love the ham of turkey.

DAVE (Patting his gun barrel) Well me an' ole Hannah sho gointer git you one. Look here, Daisy, will you choose uh bag of ground peas?

DAISY

I jus love goobers

DAVE

(Sticking out his right elbow) You lak chicken?

DAISY

Yeah

DAVE Take uh wing. (She locks arms with him and they strut inside the store.)

LIGE

Ah blieve dat fool is got some gumption. Jim Weston better watch out.

WALTER

Oh I ain't never figgered Dave was no fool. He's uh bottom fish. Jim talks all de time but Dave will run him uh hot–here he come now. (Looks off left. All look the same way.)

LUM Lawd, don't he look mean? (She chuckles) Ah bet he know Daisy's here wid Dave. Ah wouldn't take nothin' for dis.

(Enter Jim Weston left with a guitar looking very glum. He stops beside the step for a moment. Takes off his hat and fans with it.)

JIM

Howdy do, folks.

ALL

Howdy do, Jim.

JIM Don't do all they say. (He sees the gun leaning against the rail) Who gun dat? (Points at the gun)

LIGE You know so well whose gun dat is. Ah jus' heard him say he's goin out to git his gal uh ham of a turkey gobbler out round de cypress swamp. He's inside now treatin her to penders and candy. (He winks at the others and they wink back)

WALTER (Turns and calls into the store) Say, Dave! Don't try to keep Daisy in dere all day. Her feller out here waitin to scorch her home.

DAVE (from inside store)

Let him come git her if she want him.

LIGE Umph! dere now, de mule done kicked Rucker! (Calls inside to Dave) I hear you crowin, rooster. I know yo' nest aint far.

HAMBO (From inside store) Yeah, dis rooster must know something–he's gittin plenty grit in his craw.

(General laughter)

(There is a gay burst of laughter from inside the store. In a moment
Dave enters from the store with Daisy on his left arm. With his right
he is stuffing shells into his pocket. The air is tense. Lindsay,
Hambo and Joe Clarke all enter behind the couple)

DAVE (Releases Daisy and steps to the edge of the porch right in front of Jim and
looks up at the sky) Well, sun's gettin low–better git on out to de swamp and git dat
gobbler. (He turns and picks up de gun and breaks it)

JIM
Lo Daisy. (Sullenly)

DAISY (Brightly) Hello Jimmy (She is eating peanuts) Ain't Dave smart? He's
gonna kill me uh turkey an' ah kin eat all ah wants.

JIM
He aint de onliest person kin shoot round here.

LIGE Yeah, but he's best marksman just de same. Taint no use talkin, Jim. You
can't buck Dave in de woods. But you got de world beat wid uh git-fiddle. Yessuh,
Dave is uh sworn marksman but you kin really beat de box. Less have uh tune.

JIM
Oh I ain't for pickin no box. I come to git some shells for my rifle.
Sorta figgered on uh wild turkey or two. (He comes up on the porch and
starts in the store)

DAISY
If Dave go git me dat big ole turkey an' you go git me one too–gee!
Wont I have uh turkey fit?

LINDSAY
Lord, Daisy, you gointer have dese boys killin up every turkey in
Orange County.

WALTER You mean *Dave.* Jim couldn't hit de side of uh barn wid uh brass fiddle.

JIM (Hitching up his trousers) Who can't shoot? (to Clarke) Come on an' gimme
un box uh shells. I'll show yuh who kin shoot! (He exits into store with Clarke behind
him)

DAVE
(To Daisy) You wait here till ah git back wid yo' turkey.

DAISY
Ahm skeered.

DAVE Whut you skeered of? Jim? He aint no booger boo, if his ears do flop lak
uh mule.

DAISY Naw. Ah aint skeered uh no Jim. Ah got tuh git back tuh de white folks
an Ahm skeered tuh go round dat lake at night by myself. (Enter Jim from store and
stands in door with box of shells in his hand)

JIM No girl look like you don't have to go home by yo' self, if it was midnight.

DAVE
(Gun in hand and ready to exit) Naw, cause Ahm right here–

JIM Daisy don't you trust yo'self round dat lake after dark, wid dat (points at Dave)
breath and–britches. You needs uh real man to perteck you from dem 'gators and
moccasins.

DAVE
Let somethin happen and she'll find out who got rabbit blood and who aint. Well, Ahm gone. (He steps down off the steps but looks back at Daisy).

JIM Ahm goin too–git you uh great big ole turkey-rooster. (Dave takes a step or two towards left exit).

DAISY Jim, aint you gointer knock off a li'l tune fo' you go? Ahm lonesome for some music.

(Dave stops in his tracks and looks wistful. Jim sets down the shells on the bench and picks up his box with a swagger and tunes a bit.)

WALTER
Georgy Buck!

JIM (Plays the air thru once then starts to sing. Dave leans his gun against the fence and stands there.)

1.

Georgy Buck is dead, last word he said
I don't want no shortenin in my bread.

2.

Rabbit on de log–Aint got no dog
How am I goin git him, God knows.

(Dave walks on back near the step, and begins to buck a wing. Daisy comes down the step admiring both the playing and the dancing. All the men goin in singing and clapping)

3.

Rabbit on de log–aint got no dog
Shoot him wid my rifle, bam! bam!

4.

Oh Georgie Buck is dead, last word he said
Never let a woman have her way

(The tempo rises. As Dave does a good break he brings up directly in front of Daisy. He grabs her and swings her into a slow drag. The porch cheers. Jim stops abruptly. (Enter two women, right and hurry up to the porch)

1st WOMAN (LULU) Don't stop, Jim! Hit dat box a couple mo' licks so some of dese men kin scorch us in de store and treat us.

JIM
Aw, I dont feel lak no playin.

DAVE (Grinning triumphantly) Ahm gone dis time to git dat turkey. Daisy run tell yo' ma to put on de hot water kittle (He exits left with gun on shoulder)

DAISY
Oh lemme see if I got a letter in de postoffice (She exits into store)

JIM
He better git for home fore ah bust dis box over his head.

2nd WOMAN (Jenny)
(Grabbing Lige) Aw, don't worry bout Dave Carter. Play us some music

so I kin make Lige buy me some soda water. (She is playfully dragging
Lige towards the door). Jenny you grab Walter.

(Walter makes a break to jump off the porch and run. The woman catches him and
there is a very gay bit of tussling as the men are dragged towards the door)

1st WOMAN (Miss Lulu) I bet if this was Daisy, they'd uh done halted inside and
toted out half de store.

JENNY Yeah. (gets Walter to the door) Everything you hear is Daisy, Daisy, Daisy!
Just cause she got a walk on her like she done gone crazy thru de hips! (Yanks Walter
into the door) Yeah, y'all goin treat us. Come on!

WALTER
Yeah, but Daisy's uh young pullet and you gittin gray headed.

JENNY Thank God I aint gray elsewhere! Come right on. You gointer buy me
some soda water nigger. (to Jim) Play us some music, Jim, so we kin grand march up
to de counter.

JIM I can't play nothin–mad as I is. I'm one minute to boilin and two minutes to
steam. I smell blood!

MISS LULU
You don't want to fight, do you?

JIM
Sho do. You aint never seen a Weston yet dat wouldn't fight, have you?

LIGE Thats whut they all got run outa town for–fightin. (Calls into store) Hey, Joe,
give Jenny and Lulu some soda water and ground peas on me so they'll turn us loose.
(to Jim) Yeah, y'all Westons blieves in fightin.

JIM Ahd ruther get run out for fightin than to be uh coward. (He slings the guitar
round his neck an' picks up his box of shells.) Well, Ah reckon Ah'll go git Daisy her
turkey cause she sho wont git none less Ah go git it. Here come Elder Simms anyhow
now taint no mo' pickin de box. (to Daisy) Don't git lonesome whilst Ahm gone.

(Enter Daisy from the store smiling, and walks down to where Jim is standing)
DAISY
Whuts all dis talk about fightin?

JIM Lige throwin it up to me bout all my folks been run outa town for fightin. But
I don't keer!

DAISY Mah mouf done got lonesome already. Buy me some chewing gum to keep
mah mouf comp'ny till y'all gits back wid dat turkey.

JIM
Don't hafta buy none. (reaches in his pocket and pulls out a stick)
What it takes tuh satisfy de ladies, Ah totes it. (He hands her the
gum tenderly) 'By, Daisy. (He walks to left exit)

DAISY
(Coyly) Bye, till you come back.

(Enter Elder Simms right)
Good evenin' everybody.

ALL
Good evenin', Elder Sims.

LUM (Getting up from his seat on the porch) Have mah seat, Elder. Sims takes it with a sigh of pleasure. Lum steps off the porch and sets his hat over one eye) Say, Daisy, you aint goin to sprain yo' lil mouf on dat tough chewin gum, is yuh? Not wid de help *you* got. Better lemme kinda tender dat gum up for yuh so yo' lil mouf won't hafta strain wid it. (He places himself exactly in front of her. She glances up coyly at him)

DAISY Ain't you crazy, now? (Lum tries to snatch the gum but she pops it into her mouth and laughs as he seizes her hands.

LUM You don't need no gum to keep yo' mouf company wid me around. Ahm all de compny yo' mouf need. Ahm sweet papa chewin and sweetness change.

DAISY Tell dat to Bootsie Pitts, you cant fool me. (turns right) Guess Ah better go home and see mama. Ah ain't been round since Ah come from de white folk. You goin walk round there wid me?

LUM Naw, Ah aint gointer *walk*. When Ahm wid de angels ah puts on mah hosanna wings and flies round heben lak de rest. (He falls in beside her and catches her elbow) Less go! (to the porch) See you later and tell you straighter.

LINDSAY Don't stay round to Daisy's too long, Lum, and get run out from under yo' hat!

LUM
Who run?

HAMBO
Taint no use in you hollerin "who". Yo' feet don't fit no limb.
(General laughter) (Exit Lum and Daisy right)

WALTER Lawd! Daisy sho is propaganda. She really handles a lot of traffic. Ah don't blame de boys. If Ah was uh single man Ah'd be round there myself.

LIGE Ahm willin tuh serve some time on her gang as it is, but mah wife won't lissen to reason. (Laughter) Ah tries to show her dis deep point where taint right for one woman to be harboring uh whole man all to herself when theres heaps uh po' young girls aint got no husband atall. But Ah just can't sense her into it.
(Laughter)

HAMBO Now take Jim and Dave for instant. Here they is, old friends, done fell out and ready to fight—all over Daisy.

WALTER Thass me all over. I don't want no partnership when it comes to my women. Its whole hawg uh none. Lawd, what wimmen makes us do!

LINDSAY What is it dey don't make us do. Now take for instant Jim Weston. He know he can't hunt wid Dave—Dave is uh sworn marksman, but jes' so as not to be outdone here he go trying to shoot turkeys—wild turkeys mind you, 'ginst Dave.

JOE CLARKE I God, I hope he finds 'em too. If he get to killin turkeys maybe he'll stay way from my hen house. I God, I done lost nine uh my best layin' hens in three weeks.
(General Laughter)

WALTER
Did Jim git em?

CLARKE I ain't personatin' nobody but I been told dat Jim's got uh powerful lot uh chicken feathers buried in his back yard. I know one thing if I ever ketch his toe-nails in my chicken yard, I God, he's gointer follow his pappy and his four brothers. He's got to git from dis town of mine.

(Enter a little girl right, very neat and starchy. She runs up to Rev. Sims.)

GIRL Papa, mama say send her dat witch hazely oil she sent you after right quick.

LINDSAY

Whuss matter wid Sister Sims–poly today?

SIMS She don't keep so well since we been here, but I reckon she's on de mend.

HAMBO

Don't look like she never would be sick. She look so big and portly.

CLARKE Size don't mean nothin'. My wife is portly and she be's on de sick list all de time. It's "Jody, pain in de belly all day. Jody, pain in de back all night.

LIGE Besides, Mrs. Simms ain't very large. She wouldn't weigh more'n two hundred. You ain't seen no big woman. I seen one so big she went to whip her lil boy an' he run up under her belly and stayed up under dere for six months.

(General laughter)

WALTER You seen de biggest ones. But I seen uh woman so little till she could go out in uh shower uh rain and run between de drops. She had tuh git up on uh box tuh look over uh grain uh sand.

SIMMS Y'all boys better read yo' Bibles 'stead of studyin foolishness. (He gets up and starts into the store. Clarke and the little girl follow him.) Reckon Ah better git dat medicine. (The three exit into store)

HAMBO Well, y'all done seen so much–be y'all ain't never seen uh snake big as de one Ah seen down round Kissimnee. He was so big he couldn't hardly move his self. He laid in one spot so long he growed moss on him and everybody thought he was uh log layin' there; till one day Ah set down on him and went to sleep. When Ah woke up ah wuz in Middle Georgy.

(General laughter. Two women enter left and go in store after everybody has spoken to them)

LINDSAY Layin' all sides to jokes now, y'all remember dat rattlesnake Ah kilt on Lake Hope was 'most big as dat one.

WALTER

(Nudgin' Lige and winking at the crowd) How big did you say it was, Joe?

LINDSAY He mought not uh been quite as big as dat one–but jes' bout fourteen feet.

HAMBO Gimme dat lyin' snake! He wasn't but fo' foot long when you kilt him and here you done growed him ten feet after he's dead.

(Enter Simms followed by the girl with an all day sucker. Simms has a small package in his hand.

SIMMS

(Gives the package to the child and resumes his seat.)

Run 'long home now. Tell yo' ma to put on uh pot uh peas.

(Child exits right trotting and sucking her candy.)

WALTER They's some powerful big snakes round here. We was choppin' down de weeds in front of our parsonage yistiddy and kilt uh great big ol' cotton mouf moccasin.

SIMMS Yeah, look like me or some of my fambly 'bout to git snake-bit right at our own front do'.

LIGE
An' bit by uh Baptist snake at dat.

LINDSAY
How you make him out uh Baptist snake?

LIGE
Nobody don't love water lak uh Baptist an' uh Moccasin.
(General laughter)

HAMBO
An' nobody don't hate it lak de devil, uh rattlesnake an uh Meth'dis.
(General laughter. Enter Joe Clark from store. Stands in door)

SIMMS Dis town needs uh cleanin' in more ways than one. Now if this town was run right, when folks misbehaves, they oughter be locked up in jail and if they can't pay no fine, they oughter be made to work it out on de streets–chopping weeds.

LINDSAY
How we gointer do all dat when we ain't got no jail?

SIMMS Well, you orta *have* uh jail. Y'all needs uh whole heap of improvements in dis town. Ah ain't never pastored no town so way back as this one here.

CLARKE
(Stepping out before Simms) What improvements you figgers we needs?

SIMMS A whole heap. Now for one thing, we really does need uh jail, Brother Mayor. Taint no sense in runnin' people out of town that cuts up. We oughter have jails like other towns. Every town I ever pastored had uh jail.

CLARKE (Angrily) Now hold on uh minute, Simms! Don't you reckon uh man dat knows how to start uh town knows how to run it? You ain't been here long enough to find out who started dis town yet. (Very emphatic, beating of his palm with other fist) Do you know who started dis town? (Does not pause for an answer) Me! I started *dis* town. I went to de white folks and wid *dis* right hand I laid down two hundred dollars for de land and walked out and started dis town. I ain't like some folks–come here when grapes was ripe. I was here to cut new ground.

SIMMS
Well, tain't no sense in one man stayin' Mayor all de time, nohow.

CLARKE (Triumphantly) So dat de tree you barkin' up? Why, you ain't nothin' but uh trunk man. You can't be no mayor. I got roots here.

SIMMS
You ain't all de voters, tho, Brother Mayor.

CLARKE (Arrogantly) I don't hafta be. I God, it's my town and I kin be Mayor jes' as long as I want to. (Slaps his chest) I God, it was *me* dat put dis town on de map.

SIMMS What map you put it on, Brother Clarke? You musta misplaced it. I ain't seen it on no map.

CLARKE Tain't on no map, hunh? I God, everytime I go to Maitland de white folks calls me Mayor. Otherwise, Simms, I God, if you so dissatisfied wid de way I run dis town, just take yo' Bible and flat foots and git younder cross de woods.

SIMMS (Aggressively) Naw, Ah don't like it. You ack lack tain't nobody in de corporation but you? Now look. (Points at the street lamp) Tain't but one street light in town an' you got it in front of yo' place. We pays de taxes an' you got de lamp.

CLARKE
I God, nobody can't tell me how to run dis town. I 'lected myself and
I'm gonna run it to suit myself. (Looks all about) Where is dat
Marshall? He ain't lit de lamp?

WALTER
Scorched Daisy Blunt home and ain' got back.

CLARKE
I God, call him there, some of you boys.
(Lige steps to edge of porch left and calls "Lum! Lum!" Lum's voice at a distance: "What!" Lige: "Come on and light de lamp it gittin dark.")

SIMMS
Now, when I pastored in Ocala you oughter seen de lovely jail dey had.

HAMBO
Thass all right for white folks. We colored folks don't need no jail.

WALTER Aw, yes we do too. Elder Simms is right. We ain't a bit bottern white folks. (Enter the two women from the store.) You wimmen folks been in dat store uh mighty long time.

MRS. LULU
We been makin' our market.

HAMBO Looks mighty bad for some man's pocket. But y'all ain't had no treat on me. Go back and tell Mrs. Clark tuh give you some candy.

LINDSAY Have somethin' on me too. Money ain't no good lessen de women kin help you use it. (Hollers inside) Every lady in there take a treat on me.

MRS. JENNY
Ain't y'all comin' in tuh help us eat de treat. Come on, Elder Simms!

HAMBO (Getting up quickly. Lindsay and Joe Clarke also get up. They go inside laughing.) Here, lemme git hold of somebody. (Grabs one of the women by the arm as they exit into the store.)

LIGE (Pointing his thumb after the women) Ah wouldn't way lay nothin' lak dat. Too old even tuh chew peanuts if Ah was tuh buy it.

WALTER Preach it, Brother. But they's all right for mullet heads like Lindsay and Hambo. (Sings)
When they git old, when they [Note: corrected missing space.] git old
Old folks turns tuh monkeys
When they git old.
(Looks off right) Lawd! They must be havin' recess in heben! Look at dese lil ground angels! (Yells off right) Hello Big 'Oman, an' Teets and Bootsie! Hurry up! My money jumpin' up and down in my pocket lak uh mule in uh tin stable. (Enter three girls right, dressed in cool cotton dresses. They are all locked armed and giggling)

LIGE

Hello, folkses.

BOOTSIE (Coquettishly) Hello yo'self–Want uh piece uh corn bread look on de shelf. (Great burst of laughter from inside the store)

LIGE

(Catching Bootsie's arm) Lemme scorch y'all inside en' treat yuh.

BOOTSIE

(Looks at the other girls for confirmation) Not yet, after while.

WALTER

Well, come set on de piazza an' les' have some chat.

TEETS

We ain't got time. We come tuh git our mail out de postoffice.

LIGE Youse uh Got-dat-wrong! You come after Dave an' Jim an' Lum. But Daisy done treed de las' one of 'em. She got Jim and Dave out in de swamp where de mule was drugged out huntin' her uh turkey. An' she got Lum at her house. Thass how come de light ain't lit.

BIG 'OMAN

Oh, Ah ain't worried 'bout Lum. Ah b'lieve Ah kin straighten him out.

WALTER

Some wimmen kin git yo' man so he won't stand uh straightenin'.

LIGE Don't come rollin' yo' eyes at me an' gittin' all mad cause y'all stuck on de boys and de boys is stuck on Daisy. (makes a sly face at Walter)

TEETS Who? Me? Nobody ain't studyin' 'bout ole Daisy. She come before me like a gnat in a whirlwind.

WALTER (in mock seriousness) Better stop dat talkin' 'bout Daisy, do I'll tell her whut you say. I think I better call her anyhow and see whether you gointer talk dat big talk to her face. (Makes a move as if to call Daisy)

LIGE (keeping up the raillery, grabs Walter) Don't do dat, Walter. We don't want no trouble round here. But sho nuff, [Note: corrected missing space.] girls, y'all ain't got no time wid Daisy. Know what Lum say? Says Daisy is a bucket flower–jes' *made* him to set up on de porch an' look pretty. I ast him how 'bout de rest an' he says "Oh de rest is yard flowers jes' plant them any which a way.

BOOTSIE

I don't b'lieve Lum said no sich uh thing.

LIGE You tellin' dat flat–Ah knows. (Looks off left) Here come Lum, now, in uh big hurry jus' lak he ain't been gone two hours.

BIG 'OMAN Less we all go git our treat! (They start up on the porch. At that moment Hambo, Lindsay, Clarke, Simms, and the two women enter from the store.)

CLARKE (to Lige) Looks here, I God! Ain't Lum lit dat lamp yet? (Enter Lum left hurriedly. Clarke stands akimbo glaring at him. Lum fumbles for a match, strikes it and drops it. Gets another from his pocket and goes to the lamp and strikes it.) Somebody reach de numbskull uh box. (Walter hands Lum a box of the porch and he gets up on it and opens the lamp to light it.)

LUM (to Clarke) Reckon Ah better put some oil in de lamp. Tain't much in it.

CLARKE (Impatiently) Oh, that'll do! That'll do. It'll be time tuh put it out befo' you git it lit, I God.

(Lum lights the lamp. The men have resumed their seats and the women are on the ground and near right exit. Walter and Lige and the three girls are at the door about to enter the store. Lum has the box in his hand and is still under the lamp. He walks slowly towards the step, box in hand. At the step he looks off left.)

LUM Here come Dave. (All look left. Walter and Lige and the girls abandon the idea of the treat and wait for Dave)

HAMBO
But ah ain't seen no turkey yet. Dat ole gobbler's too smart for Dave.

(Enter Dave with gun over his shoulder and holding his head. A little blood is on his shoulder. He pauses under the lamp a moment then comes to the step)

HAMBO Whuss de matter, Dave? Dat ole turkey gobbler done pecked you in de head? Whut kind of a huntsman is you?

(General laughter)

DAVE Naw, ain't no turkey pecked me. It's Jim. Ah wuz out in de woods and hand don squatted down before he got dere. Ah know jus' where dat ole gobbler roost at. Soon's he hit de limb an' squatted hisself, Ah let 'im have it. He flopped his wings an' tried to fly off but here he come tumblin' down right by dem ole mule bones. Jim, he was jus' comin' up when Ah fired. So when he seen dat turkey fallin', whut do he do? He fires off his gun an' make out he kilt dat turkey. Ah beat him tuh de bird and we got tuh tusslin'. He tries tuh make *me* give him *mah* turkey so's he kin run tuh Daisy an' make out he done kilt it. So we got tuh fightin' an' Ah wuz beatin' him too till he retched down an' got de hock bone uh dat mule an' lammed me over de head an' fore Ah could git up, he done took mah turkey an' went wid it. (to Clarke) Mist Clarke Ah wants tuh swear out uh warrant ginst Jim Weston. Ahm gointer law him outa dis town, too.

SIMMS
Dat wuz uh low-down caper, Jim, cut sho nuff.

CLARKE Sho its uh ugly caper tuh cut. Come on inside, Dave, an Ah'll make out de papers. He ain't goin' to carry on lak dat in *my* town.

(Exit Dave and Clarke into de store)

LINDSAY (Jokingly to Sims) See whut capers you Meth'dis niggers'll cut–lammin' folks over de head wid mule bones an' stealin' they turkeys.

SIMMS Oh you Baptist ain't uh lot better'n nobody else. You steals an' fights too.

LINDSAY (still bantering) Yeah, but we done kotched dis Meth'dis nigger an' we gointer run him right on outa town too. Jus' wait an' see. Yeah, boy. Dat Jim'll be uh gone gator 'fore tomorrow night.

WALTER Oh, I don't know whether he's gointer be gone or not. We Meth'dis got jus' as much say-so in dis town as anybody else.

LIGE Yeah. You Baptis run yo' mouf but you don't run de town. Furthermo' we ain't heard nothin' but Dave's lie. Better wait till we see Jim an' git de straight of dis thing.

HAMBO Will you lissen at dat? Dese half-washed Christians hates de truth lak uh bed-bug hates de light. God a' mighty! (rising) Ahm goin' in an' see to it dat de

Mayor makes dem papers out right. (He exits angrily into the store. Simms and all the men rise too)

SIMMS Come on Walter, you an Lige. Less we go inside too. Dat po' boy got tuh git jestice. An' 'tween de Mayor an' dese Baptists he ain't got much chance. (They exit into the store)

1st WOMAN Come on you young gals, whut y'all wanta be hangin' round de store an' its way after black dark. Yo' mammies oughter take an frail de las' one of yuh! Come along! (The girls come downoff the porch and join the women. Loud angry voices inside the store)

2nd WOMAN
Lawd, lemme git home an' tell my husban' bout all dis. Umph! Umph!
(The women and girls exit as the men all emerge from the store. Lum comes first with the warrant in his hand. Clarke emerges last.)

CLARKE Can't have all dat fuss an' racket in my store. All of you git outside dat wants tuh fight? (He begins to close up)

SIMMS
But Brother Mayor, I said it, an' I'll say it agin, tain't right–

CLARKE (turns angrily) I God, Clarke [Hand written correction: Simms], Ah don't keer whut you say. 'Taint worth uh hill uh beans nohow. Jim is gointer be 'rested for hittin' Dave an' takin' his turkey, an' if he's found guilty he's goin' way from here. Tain't no use uh you swellin' up neither. (to Lum) Go get him, Lum, an' lock 'im in my barn an' put dat turkey under arrest too. I God, de law is gointer be law in my town. (Exit Lum with an important air.)

WALTER
Where de trial gointer be, Brother Clarke, in de hall?

CLARKE Nope, it's too little. It'll hafta be in de Baptist Church. Ah reckon dat's de bigges' place in town. Three o'clock Monday evening. Now, y'all git on off my porch tuh fuss. Lige, outen dat lamp for Lum.

(The stage goes black. The crowd is dispersing slowly. Angry voices are heard. The curtain is descending slowly. Off-stage right the voice of Lum is heard calling Daisy.)

LUM
Oh Daisy! Daisy!

DAISY (at a distance) What you want, Lum?

LUM Tell yo' mama to put on de hot water kittle. I'll be round there before long.
CURTAIN

ACT II
Scene I
SETTING: Village street scene. Huge oak tree upstage center. A house or two on backdrop. When curtain goes up Sister Lucy Taylor is seen standing under the tree trying to read a notice posted on the tree. She is painfully spelling it out. Enter Sister Thomas–a younger woman (in her thirties) at left.

SISTER THOMAS
Evenin', Sis Taylor.

SISTER TAYLOR
Evenin'. (returns to the notice)

SISTER THOMAS Whut you doin'? Readin' dat notice Joe Clarke put up 'bout de meetin'? (approaches tree)

SISTER TAYLOR Is dat whut it says? I ain't much on readin' since I had my teeth pulled out. You know if you pull out dem eye teeth you ruins yo' eye sight. (turns back to notice) Whut it say?

SISTER THOMAS
(Reading notice) The trial of Jim Weston for assault and battery on Dave Carter wid a dangerous weapon will be held at Macedonia Baptist Church on Monday November 10, at three o'clock. All are welcome–by order of J. Clarke, Mayor of Eatonville, Fla. (turning to Sister Taylor) Hit's makin' on to three now.

SISTER TAYLOR You mean its right *now*. (looks up at sun to tell time) Lemme go git ready to be at de trial–cause I'm sho going to be there and I ain't goin' to bite my tongue neither.

SISTER THOMAS I done went and crapped a mess of collard greens for supper–I better go put em on–cause Lawd knows when we goin' to git outa there–and my husband is one of them dats gointer eat don't keer whut happen. I bet if Judgment day was to happen tomorrow, he'd speck I orter fix him a bucket to carry long.

(She moves to exit right)

SISTER TAYLOR All men favors they guts, chile. But whut you think of all dis mess they got going on round here?

SISTER THOMAS
I just think its a sin and a shame before de livin justice de way dese Baptis' niggers is runnin' round here carryin' on.

SISTER TAYLOR
Oh they been puttin out they brags ever since Sat'day night bout whut they gointer do to Jim. They thinks they runs this town. They tell me Rev. Singleton preached a sermon on it yesterday.

SISTER THOMAS
Lawd help us! He can't preach and he look like 10 worth of have-mercy, let lone gittin' up dare tryin' to throw slams at us. Now all Elder Sims done was to explain to us our rights–Whut you think bout Joe Clarke running round here takin' up for those ole Baptist niggers?

SISTER TAYLOR De puzzle-gut rascal–we oughter have him up in conference and put him out de Meth'dis' faith. He don't blong in there–Wanta run dat boy outa town for nothin'.

SISTER THOMAS But we all know how come he so hot to law Jim outa town–hits to dig de foundation out from under Elder Sims–

SISTER TAYLOR
What he wanta do dat for?

SISTER THOMAS Cause he wants to be a God-knows-it-all an' a God-do-it-all and Simms is de onliest one in this town whut will buck up to him.

(Enter Sister Jones, walking leisurely)

SISTER JONES

Hello Hoyt, Hello Lucy.

SISTER TAYLOR

Goin' to de meetin'?

SISTER JONES

Done got my clothes on de line and I'm bound to be dere–

SISTER THOMAS

Gointer testify for Jim?

SISTER JONES Naw. I reckon–Don't make much difference to me which way de drop fall–Taint neither one of 'em much good.

SISTER TAYLOR I know it. I know it, Ida. But dat ain't de point. De crow we wants to pick is, is we gointer set still and let dese Baptist tell us when to plant and when to pluck up?

SISTER JONES Dat *is* something to think about when you come to think about it. (starts to move on) Guess I better go ahead–See y'all later and tell you straighter. (Enter Elder Simms right, walking fast, Bible under his arm, almost collides with Mrs. Jones. She nods and smiles and exits.)

ELDER SIMMS

How you do, Sister Taylor, Sister Thomas.

BOTH

Good evenin', Elder

SIMMS

Sho is a hot day

SISTER TAYLOR

Yeah, de bear is walkin' de earth lak a natural man.

SISTER THOMAS Reverend, look like you headed de wrong way. It's almost time for de trial and youse all de dependence we got.

ELDER SIMMS I know it. I'm trying to find de Marshall so we kin go after Jim. I wants a chance to talk wid him a minute before court sits.

SISTER TAYLOR

Y'think he'll come clear?

ELDER SIMMS (proudly) I *know* it! (shakes the Bible) I'm going to law 'em from Genesis to Revelation.

SISTER THOMAS

Give it to 'em, Elder. Wear 'em out!

ELDER SIMMS We'se liable to have a new Mayor when all dis dust settle. Well, I better scuffle on down de road.

(Exit Sims left)

SISTER THOMAS

Lord, lemme gwan home and put dese greens on. (looks off stage left)

Here come Mayor Clark now, wid his belly settin' out in front of him

like a cow-catcher. His name oughter be Mayor Belly.

SISTER TAYLOR (akimbo) Jus' look at him! Trying to look like a jigadier Breneral.

(Enter Clarke hot and perspiring. They look at him coldly.)

CLARKE I God, de bear got me! (silence for a moment) How y'all feelin' ladies?

SISTER TAYLOR Brother Mayor, I ain't one of these folks dat bite my tongue and bust my gall–Whuts inside got to come out! I can't see to my rest why you cloakin' in wid dese Baptist buzzards ginst yo' own Church.

MAYOR CLARKE

I ain't cloakin' in wid *none*. I'm de Mayor of dis whole town.
I stands for de right and against de wrong. I don't keer who it kill
or cure.

SISTER THOMAS

You think it's right to be runnin' dat boy off for nothin?

MAYOR CLARKE I God! You call knockin' a man in de head wid a mule bone nothin'? 'Nother thing–I done missed nine of my best-layin' hens. I ain't sayin' Jim got 'em–but different people has told me he buries a powerful lot of feathers in his back yard. I God, I'm a ruint man! (He starts towards the right exit, but Lum Rogers enters right.) I God, Lum, I been lookin' for you all day. It's almost three o'clock. (hands him a key from his ring) Take dis key and go fetch Jim Weston on to de church.

LUM

Have you got yo' gavel from de lodge-room?

CLARKE I God, that's right, Lum. I'll go get it from de lodge room whilst you go git de bone an' de prisoner. Hurry up! You walk like dead lice droppin' off you! (He exits right while Lum crosses stage towards left)

SISTER TAYLOR

Lum, Elder Simms been huntin' you–he's gone on down bout de barn.
(She gestures.)

LUM

I reckon I'll overtake him. (Exit left)

SISTER THOMAS I better go put dese greens on–my husband will kill me if he don't find no supper ready. Here come Mrs. Blunt. She oughter feel like a penny's worth of have-mercy wid all dis stink behind her daughter.

SISTER TAYLOR Chile, some folks don't keer. They don't raise they chillen, they drags 'em up. God knows if dat Daisy was mine, I'd throw her down and put a hundred lashes on her back wid a plow-line. Here she come in de store Sat'day night (acts coy and coquettish, burlesques Daisy's walk) a wringing and a twisting!

(Enter Mrs. Blunt left.)

MRS. BLUNT

How y'all sisters?

SISTER THOMAS

Very well, Miz Blunt, how you?

MRS. BLUNT

Oh so-so.

SISTER TAYLOR

I'm kickin' but not high.

MRS. BLUNT

Well, thank God you still on prayin' ground and in a Bible

Country–Me, I ain't many today. De niggers got my Daisy's name all mixed up in diss mess.

SISTER TAYLOR
You musn't mind dat, Sister Blunt. People just *will* talk. They's talkin' in New York and they's talkin' in Georgy and they's talkin' in Italy.

SISTER THOMAS Chile, if you talk after niggers they'll have you in de graveyard or in Chattahoochee one. You can't pay no tention to talk.

MRS. BLUNT Well, I know one thing–de man or woman, chick or child, grizzly or gray that tells me to my face anything wrong bout *my* chile–I'm going to take *my* fist (rolls up right sleeve and gestures with right fist) and knock they teeth down they throat. (She looks ferocious.) Cause y'll know I raised my Daisy right round my feet till I let her go up north last year wid them white folks. I'd ruther her to be in de white folks kitchen than walkin' de streets like some of dese girls round here. If I do say so, I done raised a lady. She can't help it if all dese men get stuck on her.

SISTER TAYLOR You'se telling de truth, Sister Blunt–that's what I always say– Don't confidence dese niggers, do they'll sho put you in de street.

SISTER THOMAS Naw indeed. Never syndicate wid niggers–do–they will distriminate you. They'll be an *anybody*. You goin to de trial, ain't you?

MRS. BLUNT Just as sho as you snore, and they better leave Daisy's name outer dis too. I done told her and told her to come straight home from her work. Naw, she had to stop by dat store and skin her gums back wid dem trashy niggers. She better not leave them white [Corrected missing space.] folks today to come praipsin over here scornin her name all up wid dis nigger mess–do, I'll kill her. No daughter of mine ain't going to do as she please long as she live under de sound of my voice. (She crosses to right.)

SISTER THOMAS That's right, Sister Blunt–I glory in yo' spunk. Lord, I better go put on my supper. (As Mrs. Blunt exits right, Rev. Singletary enters left with Dave and Deacon Lindsay and Sister Lewis. Very hostile glances from Sisters Thomas and Taylor towards the others.

ELDER SINGLETARY
Good evening, folks.

(Sister Thomas and Sister Taylor just grunt. Sister Thomas moves a step or two towards exit. Flirts her skirts and exits.)

LINDSAY
(Angrily) Whuts de matter, y'all? Cat got yo' tongue?

SISTER TAYLOR
More matter than you kin scatter all over Cincinnatti.

LINDSAY Go head on, Lucy Taylor, go head on. You know a very little of yo' sugar sweetens my coffee. Go head on. Everytime you lift yo' arm you smell like a nest of yellow hammers.

SISTER TAYLOR Go head on yo'self. Yo' head look like it done wore out three bodies–talking bout *me* smelling–you smell lak a nest of grand daddies yo'self.

LINDSAY

Aw, rack on down de road, 'oman. Ah don't wantuh change words wid yuh.
You'se too ugly.

MRS. TAYLOR You ain't nobody's pretty baby yo'self. You so ugly I betcha yo'
wife have to spread uh sheet over yo' head tuh let sleep slip up on yuh.

LINDSAY (Threatening) You better git 'way from me while you able. I done tole
you I don't wants break a mouth wid you. It's a whole heap better tuh walk off on yo
own legs than it is to be toted off. I'm tired of yo' achin round here. You fool wid me
now an' I'll knock you into doll rags, Tony or no Tony.

SISTER TAYLOR (jumping up in his face) Hit me! Hit me! I dare you tuh hit me.
If you take dat dare you'll steal a hawg an' eat his hair.

LINDSAY

Lemme gwan down to dat church befo' you make me stomp you.
(He exits right.)

SISTER TAYLOR You mean you'll *git* stomped. Ahm going to de trial too. De
nex trial gointer be *me* for kickin some uh you Baptis niggers around.

(A great noise is heard off stage left. The angry and jeering voices of children.
Mrs. Taylor looks off left and takes a step or two towards left exit as the noise comes
nearer.)

VOICE OF ONE CHILD Tell her! Tell her! Turn her up and smell her. Yo' mama
ain't got nothin to do wid me.

SISTER TAYLOR (Hollering off left) You lil Baptis haitians, leave them chillun
alone. If you don't, you better!

(Enter about 10 chidren struggling and wrestling in a bunch. Mrs. Taylor looks
about on the ground for a stick to strike the children with.)

VOICE OF CHILD IN CROWD

Hey! Hey! He's skeered tuh knock it off. Coward!

SISTER TAYLOR

If y'all don't git on home!

SASSY LITTLE GIRL (Standing akimbo) I know you better not touch me, do my
mama will tend to you.

SISTER TAYLOR (Making as if to strike her) Shet up, you nasty lil heifer, sassing
me! You ain't half raised.

(The little girl shakes herself at Mrs. Taylor and is joined by two or three others.)

SISTER TAYLOR (Walking towards right exit) I'm going on down to de church
an' tell yo' mammy. But she ain't been half raised herself. (She exits right with
several children making faces behind her.)

A BOY (to sassy girl) Aw haw! Y'all ol' Baptis ain't got no book case in yo'
church. We went there one day an' I saw uh soda cracker box settin' up in de corner
so I set down on it. (pointing at sassy girl) Know whut ole Mary Ella say? (jeering
laughter) Willie, you git up off our library! Haw! Haw!

MARY ELLA

Y'all ole Meth'dis' ain't got no window panes in yo' ole church.

A GIRL (Takes center of stage and hands akimbo shakes her hips.) I don't keer whut y'allsay. I'm a Methdis' bred an' uh Methdis' born an' when I'm dead there'll be uh Methdis' gone.

MARY ELLA (snaps fingers under other girl's nose and starts singing. Several join her.)

Oh Baptis, Baptis is my name
My name's written on high
I got my lick in de Baptis church
Gointer eat up de Methdis pie

(the Methodist children jeer and make faces. The Baptist camp make faces back for a full minute there is silence while each camp tries to outdo the other in face making. The Baptist makes the last face.

METHODIST BOY Come on, less us don't notice em. Less gwan down to de church an' hear de trial.

MARY ELLA
Y'all ain't the onliest ones kin go. We goin' too.

WILLIE Aw Haw! Copy cats! (Makes face) Dat's right, follow on behind us lak uh puppy dog tail. (They start walking toward right exit switching their clothes behind.)

(Baptist children stage a rush and struggle to get in front of the methodists. They finally succeed in flinging some of the Methodist children to the ground and some behind them and walk towards right exit haughtily switching their clothes.)

WILLIE (whispers to his crowd) Less go round by Mosely's lot and beat 'em there!

OTHERS
All right!

WILLIE
(Yelling to Baptists) We wouldn't walk behind no ole Baptists! (The Methodists turn and walk off towards left exit switching their clothes as the Baptists are doing.)

SLOW CURTAIN
ACT II
SCENE II
SETTING: Interior of Macedonia Baptist Church, a rectangular room, windows on each side, two "Amen Corners", pulpit with a plush cover with heavy fringe, practical door in pulpit, practical door in front of church, two oil brackets with reflectors on each side wall with lamps missing all but one, one big oil lamp in center.

ACTION: At the rise, church is about full. A buzz and hum fills the church. Voices of children angry and jeering heard from the street. The church bell begins to toll for death. Everybody looks shocked.

SISTER LEWIS
Lawd! Is Dave done died from dat lick?

SISTER THOMAS (to her husband) Walter, go see. (He gets up and starts down the aisle to front door. Enter Deacon Hambo by front door.)

WALTER
Who dead?[Note: correction to e]

HAMBO (laughing) Nobody–jus' tollin' de bell for dat Meth'dis gopher dat's gointer be long long gone after dis trial. (laughter from the Baptist side)

WALTER Y'all sho thinks you runs dis town, dontcher? But Elder Simms'll show you somethin' t'day. If he don't, God's uh gopher.

HAMBO

He can't show us nothin' cause he don't know nothin' hisself.

WALTER

He got mo' book-learnin' than Rev. Singletary got.

HAMBO He mought be unletter-learnt, but he kin drive over Sims like a road plow.

METHODIST CHORUS

Aw, naw! Dat's a lie!

(Enter Rev. Simms by front door with open Bible in hand. A murmur of applause arises on the Methodist side, grunts on the Baptist side. Immediately behind him comes Lum Boger leading Jim Weston. They parade up to the right Amen Corner and seat themselves on the same bench, Jim between the Marshall and the preacher. A great rooster crowing and hen cackling arises on the Baptist side. Jim Weston jumps angrily to his feet.)

(Enter by front door Rev. Singletary and Dave. Dave's head is bandaged, but he walks firmly and seems not ill at all. They sit in the left Amen Corner. Jeering grunts from the Methodist side.)

SISTER THOMAS

Look at ol' Dave trying to make out he's hurt.

LIGE Everybody know uh Baptis' head is hardern uh rock. Look like they'd be skeered tuh go in swimmin', do they heads would drown 'em. (general laughter on Methodist side)

(Enter Bro. Nixon with his jumper jacket on his arm and climbs over the knees of a bench full of people and finds seat against the wall directly beneath empty lamp bracket. He looks around for some place to dispose of his coat. Sees the lamp-bracket and hangs up the coat, hitches up his pants and sits down.)

SISTER LEWIS (rising and glaring at Nixon) Shank Nixon, you take yo' lousy coat down off these sacred walls. Ain't you Methdis' niggers got no gumption in de house of Wash-up!

(Nixon mocks her by standing akimbo and shaking himself like a woman. General laughter. He prepares to resume his seat but looks over and sees Deacon Hambo on his feet, and glaring angrily at him. He quickly reaches up and takes the coat down and folds it across his knees.)

(Sister Taylor looks very pointedly at Sister Lewis then takes a dip of snuff and looks sneering at Lewis again.)

SISTER TAYLOR

Some folks is a whole lot more keerful bout a louse in de church than
Note: corrected missing space

they is in they house. (Looks pointedly at Sister Lewis.)

SISTER LEWIS (bustling) Whut you gazin' at me for? Wid your pop-eyes looking like skirt ginny-nuts.

SISTER TAYLOR I hate to tell you whut yo' mouf looks like. I sho do you and soap and soap and water musta had some words.

SISTER LEWIS Talkin' bout other folks being dirty–yo' young 'uns must be sleep in they draws cause you kin smell 'em a mile down de road.

SISTER TAYLOR
Taint no lice on 'em though.

SISTER LEWIS You got just as many bed-bugs and chinches as anybody else, don't come trying to hand me dat rough package bout yo' house so clean.

SISTER TAYLOR Yeah, but I done seen de bed-bugs munchin' out yo' house in de mornin', keepin' step just like soldiers drillin'. An' you got so many lice I seen em on de dish-rag. One day you tried to pick up de dish-rag and put it in de dish water and them lice pulled back and tole you "Aw naw, damned if I'm going to let you drown me." (Loud laughter from the Methodist side)

SISTER LEWIS (furious–rises akimbo) Well, my house might not be exactly clean, but there's no fly-specks on my character! They didn't have to sit de sheriff to make Willie marry *me* like they did to make Tony marry *you*.

SISTER TAYLOR (Jumping up and starts across the aisle. She is pulled back out of the aisle by friends.) Yeah, they got de sheriff to make Tony marry me, but he married me and made me a good husband, too. I sits in my rocking cheer on my porch every Sat'day evening and say "here come Tony and them–

SISTER LEWIS
Them what?

SISTER TAYLOR Them dollars. Now you sho orter go git de sheriff and a shot-gun and make some of dese men marry yo' daughter Ada.

SISTER LEWIS (Jumping up and starting across the aisle. She is restrained, but struggles hard.) Lemme go, Jim Merchant! Turn me go! I'm going to stomp de black heifer till she can't sit down.

SISTER TAYLOR (Also struggling) Let her come on! If I get my hands on her I'll turn her every way but loose.

SISTER LEWIS Just come on out dis church, Lucy Taylor. I'll beat you on everything you got but yo' tongue and I'll bit dat a lick if you stick it out. (to the men holding her) Turn me go! I'm going to fix her so her own mammy won't know her. She ain't going to slip *me* into de dozens and laugh about it.

SISTER TAYLOR (Trying to free herself) Why don't y'all turn dat ole twist mouth 'oman loose. All I wants to do is hit her one lick. I betcha I'll take her 'way from here faster than de word of God.

SISTER LEWIS (to men holding Mrs. Taylor) I don't see how come y'all want let ole flat-behind Lucy Taylor aloose–make out she so bad, now. She may be red hot but I kin cool her. I'll ride her just like Jesus rode a jackass.

(They have subsided into their seats again, but are glaring at each other. Enter Mayor Clarke thru the pulpit door and is annoyed at the clamor going on. He tries to quell the noise with a frown.)

SISTER TAYLOR Dat ain't nothin' but talk–You looks lak de Devil before day, but you ain't so bad–not half as bad as you smell.

CLARKE
Order, please. Court is set.

SISTER LEWIS You looks like all hell and de devil's doll baby, but all I want *you* to do is to hit de ground and I'll crawl you. Put it where I kin git it and I'll sho use it.

MAYOR CLARKE (feeling everywhere for the gavel) Lum Boger! Where's dat gavel I told you to put here?

LUM (from beside prisoner) You said *you* were going to git it yo'self.

CLARKE I God, Lum, you gointer stand there like a bump on a log and see I ain't got nothin' to open court wid? Go head–fetch me dat gavel. Make haste quick before dese wimmen folks tote off dis church house. (Lum exits by front door)

SISTER TAYLOR (to Lewis) Aw, shut up, you big old he-looking rascal you! Nobody don't know whether you'se a man or a woman.

CLARKE
You wimmen, shut up!

SISTER LEWIS (to Taylor) Air Lawd! Dat ain't *yo* trouble. They all *knows* whut *you* is–eg-zackly!

LINDSAY Aw, why don't you wimmen cut dat out in de church-house! Jus' jawin' and chewin' de rag!

SISTER TAYLOR Joe Lindsay, if you'd go home and feed dat raw-boned horse of yourn you wouldn't have so much time to stick yo' bill in business that ain't yourn.

LINDSAY You ain't got nairn to feed–You better go hunt another dead dog and git some mo' teeth. Great big ole empty mouf, and no cheers in de parlar.

SISTER TAYLOR I kin git all de teeth I wants–I'd ruther not have no cheers in my parlor than to have them ole snags you got in yo' mouf. I'd ruther gum it out.

LINDSAY You don't *ruther* gum it out, you *hafta* gum it out. You ain't got no teeth. Dey better send out to dat ole mule and git you some teethes.

SISTER LEWIS Joe Lindsay, don't you know no better than to strain wid folks ain't got sense enough to tote guts to a bean? If they ain't born wid no sense you cna't learn 'em none.

LINDSAY You sho done tole whut God love now. (Glaring across the aisle) Ain't got enough gumption to kill a buzzard.

(Enter Lum by front door with gavel in one hand and mule bone in the other. He walks importantly up the aisles and hands Clarke the gavel and lays the bone atop the pulpit.)

CLARKE (rapping sharply with gavel) Here! You moufy wimmen shut up. (to Lum) Lum, go on back there and shut dem wimmen up or put 'em outa here.

(Lum starts walking importantly down the aisle towards Sister Taylor. she almost rises to meet him.)

SISTER TAYLOR Lum Boger, you fresh little snot you! Don't you dast to come here trying to put *me* out–Many diapers as I done pinned on *you*! Git way from me befo' I knock every nap off of yo' head, one by one.

(Lum hurries away from her apologetically. He turns towards Mrs. Lewis.)

MRS. LEWIS Deed Godknows you better not lay de weight of yo' hand on *me*, Lum. Here you ain't dry behind de ears yert and come telling *me* what to do. Gwan way from here before I kick yo' clothes up round you' neck like a horse collar.

(Lum goes on back and takes his seat beside the prisoner.)

CLARKE (glaring ferociously) This court is set and I'm bound to have some order or else. (The talking ceases. Absolute quiet)

CLARKE Now less git down to business. We got folks in dis town dat's just like a snake in de grass.

SISTER BOGER Brother Mayor! We ain't got no business going into no trial nor northin' else 'thout a word of prayer–to be sure de right spirit is wid us.

VOICE ON METHODIST SIDE Thass right,–Elder Simms, give us a word of prayer. (He rises hurriedly.)

VOICE ON BAPTIST SIDE This is a Baptist Church and de pastor is settin' right here–how come he can't pray in his own church?

VOICE ON METHODIST SIDE Y'all done started all dis mess–how you going to git de right spirit here? Go head, Rev. Simms.

VOICE ON BAPTIST SIDE
He can't pray over me. Dis Church says one Lord, one faith, one
Baptism–and a man that ain't never been baptised atall ain't got no
business praying over nobody.

CLARKE (rapping with gavel) Less sing! Somebody raise a tune.

(VOICE ON BAPTIST SIDE begins "Onward Christian Soldiers" and the others join in.)

(VOICE ON METHODIST SIDE begins "All hail the power of Jesus name" and the Methodists join in. Both shout as loud as they can to the end of the verse.)

(Mayor Clarke raps loudly for order at the end of the verse and lifts his hands as if to bless a table)

CLARKE (praying) Lord be withus and bless these few remarks we are about to receive, Amen. Now this court is open for business. All of us know we came here on serious business. This town is bout to be tore up by back-biting and malice. Now everybody that's a witness in this case stand up. I wants the witness to take the front seat.

(Nearly everybody in the room rises. Brother Hambo frowns across the aisle at Mrs. McDuffy, who is standing.)

BROTHER HAMBO
Whut *you* doing standin' up for a witness? I know you wasn't there.
You don't know one thing about it.

SISTER McDUFFY I got just as much right to testify as you is. I don't keer if I wasn't there. Any man that treat they wife bad as *you* can't tell nobody else they eye is black. You clean round yo' *own* door before you go sweeping round other folks.

SISTER LINDSAY (to Nixon) What you doin' up there testifying? When you done let yo' hawg root up all my p'tater patch.

NIXON
Aw shut up woman–You ain't had no taters for no pit to root up.

SISTER LINDSAY Who ain't had no taters? (To Lige) Look here, Lige, didn't I git a whole crokus sack full of tater slips from yo' brother Sam?

LIGE (reluctantly) Yeah.

SISTER LINDSAY Course I had sweet p'taters! And if you stand up there and tell *me* I ain't had no p'taters I'll be all over you just like gravy over rice.

NIXON
Aw shut up–We ain't come here to talk about yo' tater vines, we come–

SISTER LINDSAY (to her husband) Joe! What kind of a husband is you? Set here and let Nixon 'buse me out lak dat!

WALTER How is he going to give anybody a straightening when he needs straightening hisself. I bought a load of compost from him and *paid for it in advance* and he come there when I wasn't home and dumped a half-a-load in there and drove on off wid my money.

SISTER HAMBO Aw, you ain't got no right to talk, Walter, not low down as you is–if somebody stump their toe in dis town you won't let yo' shirt-tail touch you till you bolt over to Maitland and puke yo' guts to de white folks–and God knows I 'bominates a white folks nigger.

WALTER Aw you just mad cause I wouldn't let your old starved-out cow eat up my cow-peas.

SISTER HAMBO (triumphantly) Unhumh! I knowed you was the one knocked my cow's horn off! And you lied like a doodle-bug going backwards in his hole and made out you didn't do it.

WALTER
I didn't do no such a thing.

SISTER HAMBO
I say you did and belong to Macedonia Baptist Church and I can't lie.

WALTER Yo' mouf is cut cross ways, ain't it? Well then, yo' mouf ain't no prayer-book even if yo' lips do flap like a Bible. You kin lie and then re-lie.

DEACON HAMBO Walter Thomas talk dat biggity talk to me, not to my wife. Maybe you kin whip her, but if you can't whip me too, don't bring de mess up.

CLARKE (rapping) Y'all men folks shut up before I put you both under arrest. Come to order everybody.

LINDSAY I just wants say this before we go any further. Nobody bet not slur my wife in here–do I'll strow 'em all over de county.

MRS. NIXON Aw, youse de nastiest threatener in three states but I ain't seen you do nothin'. De seat of yo' pants is too close to de ground for you to be crowin' so loud. You so short you smell right earthy.

MRS. LINDSAY De seat of yo' husband's britches been draggin' de ground ever since I knowed him. Don't like it dontcher take it, here's my collar come and shake it. (She puts the palms of her hands together and holding the heels together, flaps the fore part of her hands like a gator opening and shutting its mouth. This infuriates Mrs. Nixon.

CLARKE Shut up! We didn't come here to wash and iron niggers. We come here for a trial. (raps)

MRS. NIXON (to Clarke) I ain't going to shut up nothin' of de kind. Think I'm going to let her low-rate me and I take it all? Naw indeed. I'm going to sack dis female out before we any further go.

MRS. LINDSAY Aw, I done dished you out too many times. Go head on and try to keep yo' lil squatty husband away from down on de lake wid wimmens and you'll have *all* you can do. How does old heavy-hipted mama talk?

(snaps her fingers)

MRS. NIXON Nobody wouldn't have you if he could get anybody else. (She makes a circle with her thum and first finger and holds it up for Mrs. Lindsay to see.) Come thru–don't you feel cheap?

CLARKE
Sister Nixon, shut up!

SISTER NIXON You can't shut me up, not the way you live. When you quit beatin Mrs. Mattie and dominizing her all de time then you kin tell other folks what to do. You ain't none of my boss. Don't let yo' wooden God and corn-stalk Jesus fool you now. Now de way you sells rancid bacon for fresh.

NIXON
Aw, honey, hush a while, please and less git started.

(A momentary quiet falls on the place. Mayor glowers all over the place. Turns to Lum.)

CLARKE Lum, git a piece of paper and a pencil and take de names of all de witnesses *who was dere while de fight was going on.*

LUM (Pulling a small tablet and pencil out of his coat pocket) I brought it with me.

CLARKE Now everybody who was at de fight hold up yo' hands so Lum can know who you are.

(Several hands go up. Sister Anderson puts up her hand.)

CLARKE
You wasn't there, Sister Anderson, not at that time.

SISTER ANDERSON I hadn't been gone more'n ten minutes 'fore Dave come in from de woods.

CLARKE
But you didn't see it.

SISTER ANDERSON It don't make no difference–my husband heered every word was spoke and told me jes' lak it happen. Don't tell *me* I can't testify.

DEACON HAMBO Nobody can't testify but de two boys cause nobody wuz at de fight but dem.

SISTER ANDERSON Dat's all right too, Brother, but I know whut they wuz fightin' about an' it wudn't no turkey neither. It wuz Daisy Blunt.

MRS. BLUNT Just you take my chile's name right out yo' mouf, Becky Anderson. She wuznt out in dat cypress swamp. Leave her out dis mess.

REV. SIMMS You ain't got no call to be so touchous bout yo' girl, but you sho said a mouthful, Sister Blunt. Dis sho is a mess. Can't help from being uh mess. (glares at Mayor) Holdin' a trial in de Baptist Church! Some folks ain't got sense enough todo 'em till four o'clock and its way after half past tree right now.

MAYOR Shet up, dere, Simms! Set down! Who ast yo' pot to boil, nohow! Court is de best church they is, anyhow, cause you come in court. You better have a good experience and a strong determination. (raps vigorously) Now lemme tell *y'all* something. When de Mayor sets Court–don't keer when I sets it nor where I sets it, you got to git quiet and stay quiet till I ast you tuh talk. I God, you sound lak a tree full uh blackbirds! Dis ain't no barbecue, nor neither no camp meetin'. We 'sembled here tuh law uh boy on a serious charge. (A great buzz rises from the congregation. Mayor raps hard for order and glares all about him.) Hear! Hear! All of us kin sing at de same time, but can't but one of us talk at a time. I'm doin' de talkin' now, so de rest of you dry up till I git through. I God, you sound lak uh passle uh dog fights! We ain't here for no form and no fashion and no outside show to de world. Wese here to law. (to Lum) You done got all de witnesses straight–Got they names down?

LUM

Yessuh, I got it all straightened out.

CLARKE

Well, read de names out and let de witnesses take de front seats.

LUM

Mr. Clarke, I done found out nobody wasn't at dat fight but Jim and
Dave and de mule bones. Dere's de bone Dave got hit wid up on de
rostrum and deres Jim and Dave in de Amen Corners.

DAVE (rising excitedly) Mist' Clarke! Brother Mayor, I wants to ast uh question right now to git some information.

MAYOR

All right, Dave, go head and ast it.

DAVE

Brother Mayor, I wanted to know whut become of my turkey gobbler?

MAYOR I God, Dave, youse in order. Lum! I God, I been layin' off to ast you whut you dont wid dat turkey. Where is it?

(A burst of knowing laughter from the house)

LUM (very embarrassed) Well, when you tole me to go 'rrest Jim and de turkey, I took and went on round to his ma's house and he wudnt dere so I took and turnt round and made it t'wards Daisy's house an' I caught up wid him under dat China-berry tree jest befo' you gits tuh Daisy's house. He was makin' it on t'wards her house wid de turkey in one hand–his gun crost his shoulder when I hailed 'im. I hollered "Jim, hold on dere uh minute!" He dropped de turkey and wheeled and throwed de gun on me.

MAYOR CLARKE

I God, he drawed uh gon on de City Marshall?

LUM Yessir! He sho did. Thought I was Dave. Tole me: "Don't you come another step unless you want to see yuh Jesus." I hollered back "It's me, I ain't no Dave Carter." So he took de gun offa me and I went up to him and put him under arrest, and locked him up in yo' barn and brought *you* de key, didn't I?

CLARKE

You sho did, but I God, I ast you whut become of de turkey?

LUM De turkey wasn't picked or nothin', so I put him under 'rrest too, jus' lak you tole me. (general laughter)

CLARKE I God, Lum, whut did you *do* wid de turkey after you put him under 'rrest?

LUM Jim, he didn't want to come wid me till he could make it to Daisy's house to give her det turkey but, bein so close up on him till he couldn't draw his rifle, I throwed my 32:20 in his face an' tole him I said "Don't you move! Don't you move uh pig do I'll burn you down! I got my burner cocked dead in yo' face and I'll keer you down jus' lak good gas went up. Come on wid me!" So I took his rifle and picked up de turkey and marched him off to yo' cow-lot. Ast him didn't I do it. I tole him, I said "I know you Westons goes for bad but I'm yo' match. I said you may be slick but you kin stand another greasing. Now sir! I ain't skeered uh nobody. I'll put de whole town under 'rrest.

MAYOR CLARKE I God, Lum, if you don't tell me whut you done wid dat turkey, you better! (draws back the gavel as if to hurl it at Lum) I'll lam you over de head wid dis mallet! Whut did you do wid dat gobbler turkey?

LUM Being as he wasn't picked or nothin', I know you didn't want to be bothered wid it, so I took and carried it over to Mrs. Blunt's house and she put on some hot water and we set up way Sat'day night pickin de turkey and fixin him so nex' day she cooked him off–just sorta baked him wid a lil stuffin an' such, so he'd keep.

MAYOR CLARKE Didn't you know my wife knowed how to cook? Go fetch dat turkey here, and don't let no dead lice fall off of you on de way.

LUM (extremely embarrassed) I don't speck he's dere now, Mist' Clarke.

CLARKE (ferociously) How come?

LUM I passed by dere on Sunday and et a lil piece of shoulder offa him, an' being everybody else was eatin' turkey too, I et some breast meat an' uh mouf ful or two of stuffin' an' uh drum stick wid de ham part of de leg hung on to it wid a lil gravy. (general laughter) I thought I was doin' right cause [Note: corrected missing space] de turkey was kilt for Daisy anyhow. So I jus' took it on to her. Dave was all hurt up and Jim was locked up so–

CLARKE
Dat'll do! Dat'll do! Dry up, Suh! (turns to Dave) Stand up, Dave.
Since youse de one got hurted, you be de first witness and tell me
just whut went on out dere.

(Dave rises slowly.)

SISTER TAYLOR Dat's right, Dave. Git up dere and lie lak de cross ties from New York to Texas. You greasy rascal you! You better go wash yo'self before you go testifying on people.

DAVE
I'm just as clean as you.

REV. SINGLETARY (jumping to his feet) Wait a minute! Taint none of y'all got no call to be throwin' off on dis boy. He come here to git justice, not to be slurred and low-rated. He ain't 'ssaulted nobody. He ain't stole no turkeys *nor* chickens. He's a clean boy. He set at my feet in Sunday school since he was so high, (measures knee height) and he come thru religion under de sound of my voice an' I baptized him and I know he's clean.

SISTER TAYLOR

It'll take more'n uh baptizin' to clean dat nigger.

DAVE I goes in swimmin' nearly every day. I'm just as clean as anybody else.

SISTER TAYLOR (Mayor begins rapping for order. She shouts out) Swimmin! Dat ain't gointer clean de crust offa *you*. You ain't had a good bath since de devil was a hatchet. If you ain't been parboiled in de wash pot and scoured wid Red Seal lye, don't bring de mess up.

CLARKE

I'm goin' to have order here or else! Gwan, Dave.

DAVE

It's just lak I tole you Sat'day night.

CLARKE Yeah, but dat wuz at de store. Dis is in [Note: corrected missing space] court and it's got to be tole agin.

ELDER SIMMS Just uh minute, Brother Clarke, before we any further go I wants to ast de witness uh question dat oughter be answered before he open his mouf.

MAYOR CLARKE

Whut *kind* of a question is dat?

SIMMS Dave, tell de truth. Ain't yo' heart full of envy and malce 'gainst dis chile? (Gestures towards Jim. Dave shakes his head and starts to deny the charge but Simms hurries on.) Wait a minute now! Wait till I git thru. Didn't y'all used to run around everywhere playin' and singing andeverything till you got so full of envy and malce and devilment till y'al broke up? Now, Brother Mayor, make him tell de truth.

DAVE Yeah, I useter be crazy bout Jim, and we was buddies till he tried to back bite me wie, wid my girl.

JIM Never *was* yo girl. Nohow I ain't none of yo' buddy. I ain't got no buddy. They kilt my buddy tryin' to raise me. But I did useter lak you till you acted so low down tryin' to undermine me and root me out wid my girl.

MAYOR Aw, table dat business an' less open up new business. We ain't here to find out whose girl it is. We wants to know 'bout dis fight and who hit de first lick and how come. Go head on Dave and talk.

DAVE Well, jus lak I tole yuh, Sat'day night, I been watchin' dat flock uh wild turkeys ever since way last summer roostin' in de edge of dat cypress swamp out by Howell Creek, where Brazzle's ole mule was dragged out. It was a great, bit ole gobbler leadin' de flock. So last time I seen him I said I was gointer git him for my girl if it taken me uh year. So Sat'day, kinda late, I grabs ole Hannah, my gun, I calls her Old Hannah, and come to de store to buy some shells. Y'all know whut went on at de store. Well, it made me feel lak I wuz gointergit dat ole gobbler if I had to follow him clean to Diddy war Diddy or slap into Ginny-Gall. But I didn't have to do nothin'. When I got out by de ole mule bones, I seen 'em flyin' round lak buzzards. So I loaded both barrels, squatted down on uh log where I had dead aim on dat big ole cypress pine where they roosts at. Sho nuff, soon's de sun had done set, here dey come followin' de leader'. He lit way out on de end of de limb kinda off from de rest and I eased ole Hannah up on him. Man! I got so skeered I wuz gointer miss him till I got de all overs. He gobbled two three times to see if all his fambly was safed den he settled down and bam! I let him have it! He spread his wings lak he wuz gointer fly on off an' I *cried* lak a chile! But I got him alright and down he come floppin, and me grabbin him before he quit kickin. Gee, I was proud. He felt lak he weighed forty pounds. Whilst I was kinda heftin him in my hands I heard uh rifle fire and I looked and dere was Jim firin into de turkey flock dat was flyin round skeered. He didn't hit a God's thing, but he seen me wid my gobbler and come runnin up talking bout give him his turkey. I ast him "who turkey you talkin bout?[Note: missing double quote?] He says dat one of hisn I hed done grabbed. I tole him he must gone crazy in de head. He says, I better give him his turkey before he beat my head off. I tole him I wasn't gointer give nobody but Daisy Blunt dat turkey. Otherwise, if he wanted to try my head, I wasn't runnin uh damn step. Come on. So he jumped on me and tried to snatch de turkey. We fit all over de place. First we was just tusslin for de bird, but when he found out he couldn't take it he hit me wid his fist. Den I ups wid my African soup bone and I bet I plowed up uh acre uh bushes wid his head. He hit ker-bam! right in dat pack uh mule bones and I turnt and started off, when lo and behold, he gits up wid dat hock bone and lams me in de head and when I come to, him and my turkey was gone. So I come swore out uh warrant against him cause didn't fight fair. I ain't mad. I always lakted Jim, but he sho done dirty—lammin me wid uh mule bone and takin' [Note: corrected missing space] my turkey.

(Dave resumes his seat and Jim drops his head for a moment, then snatches it up arrogantly and glares at the Baptists. The whole place is very silent for a moment. Then Mayor Clarke clears his throat, raps with his gavel and looks sternly at Jim.)

CLARKE Jim Weston, stand up suh! (Jim rises sullenly.) Youse charged wid 'saulting Dave Carter wid uh dangerous weapon and then stealin his lawful turkey gobbler. You heard de charge—guilty or not guilty?

JIM (arrogantly) Yeah, I hit him and I'll hit him agin if he crowd me. But I ain't guilty uh no crime. (He hitches up his pants and sits down arrogantly.)

CLARKE (surprised) Whuts dat you say, Jim? (raps sharply) Git up from there sir! Whuts dat you say?

JIM (rising) I say, heah, I lammed ole Dave wid de mule bone, but I ain't guilty uh nothin.

(There is a stark silence for a few seconds. Then Clarke raps nervously.)

CLARKE
How come you ain't guilty?

(Jim sits down amid jubilant smiles of Methodists. Simms chuckles out loud and wipes his face with his handkerchief. He gets to his feet still gloating.)

SIMMS (to Jim) Set down, Jim, and lemme show dese people dat walks in de darkness wid sinners an' republicans de light.

SINGLETARY You just as well tuh hush up befo' you start, then, Simms. You can't show nobody uh light when you ain't got none tuh show.

HAMBO
Ain't dat de gospel?

NIXON Aw, let de man talk. Y'all sound lak uh tree full uh blackbirds. Go head on, Elder Simms.

WALTER Yeah, you can't teach 'em nothin' but talk on. We know whut you talkin' about.

CLARKE (raps once or twice) I God, tell it. Whut ever tis you got tuh tell.

SISTER LEWIS An yeah, hurry up and tell it. I know it ain't goin' tuh be nothin' after you git it told but hurry up and say it so yo' egg-bag kin rest easy.

WALTER

Aw shut up an' give de man uh chance.

SISTER LEWIS

My shetters ain't workin' good. Sposin' you come shet me up, Walter.
Den you'll know it's done right.

LIGE

Aw, whyn't y'all ack lak folks an' leave de man talk.

CLARKE (rapping repeatedly) Order in dis court, I God, jus' like you was in Orlando! (Silence falls.) Now, Simms, talk yo' chat.

SIMMS (glances down into his open Bible then looks all around the room with great deliberation. It is evident he enjoys being the center of attraction. He smiles smugly as he turns his face towards the pulpit. He speaks slowly and accents his words so that none will be lost on his audience.) De Bible says, be sho' you're right, then go ahead. (He looks all around to collect the admiration he feels he has earned.) Now, we all done gethered and 'sembled here tuh law dis young lad of uh boy on uh might serious charge. Uh whole passle of us is rarin tuh drive him way from home lak you done done off his daddy an' his brothers.

HAMBO We never drove off his pappy. De white folks took an' hung him for killin' dat man [Note: corrected missing space?] in Kissimmee for nothin'.

SIMMS

Dat ain't de point, brother Hambo.

HAMBO

It's jes' as good uh point as any. If you gointer talk–tell de truth.
An if you can't tell de truth, set down an' leave Rev. Singletary
talk.

SIMMS Brother Mayor, how come you let dese people run they mouf lak uh passle uh cow-bells? Ain't I got de floor? I ain't no breath-and-britches. I was *people* in Middle Georgy befo' I ever come to Floridy. Whut kind of Chairman is you, nohow?

CLARKE (angrily) Heah! Heah! Don't you come tryin' show yo'self round me! I God, I don't keer whut you wuz in Georgy. I God, I kin eat fried chicken when you [Note: corrected missing spaces] caint git rain water tuh drink. Hurry up an' say dat mess you got in yo' craw an' set down. We needs yo' space more than we needs yo' comp'ny.

NIXON Don't let him skeer you, Elder Sims. You got plenty shoulders tuh back yo' fallin.

HAMBO

Well, each an' every shoulder kin hit de ground an' I'll git wid 'em.
Don't like it dontcher take, here my collar come an' shake it.

WALTER Hambo, everybody in Orange County knows you love tuh fight. But dis is uh law hearin'–not no wrassle.

HAMBO

Oh you Methdis' niggers wants tuh fight bad enough, but youse skeered.

Youse jus' as hot as Tucker when de mule kicked his mammy. But you know you got plenty coolers.

SISTER TAYLOR Aw, taint nobody skeered uh you half-pint Baptists. God knows Ahm ready an' willin'. (She glares at Mrs. Lewis.)

(Sister Lewis jumps to her feet but is pulled back into her seat. Mayor Clarke raps for order and the room gets quiet.)

CLARKE

Aw right now, Simms. I God, git through.

SIMMS (pompously) Now, y'all done up an' took dis po' boy an' had him locked up in uh barn ever since Sat'day night an' done got him 'coused uh assault an' stealing uh turkey an' I don't know whut all an' you ain't got no business wid yo' hands on him stell. He ain't done no crime, an' if y'all knowed anything 'bout law, I wouldn't have tuh tell you so.

CLARKE

I God, he is done uh crime and he's gointer ketch it, too.

SIMMS But not by law, Brother Mayor. You tryin' tuh lay uh hearin' on dis boy an' you can't do it cause he ain't broke no law—I don't keer whut he done so long as he don't break no law you can't tetch him.

SINGLETARY

He committed assault, didn't he? Dat sho is breakin' de law.

SIMMS Naw, he ain't committed no 'sault. He jus' lammed Dave over de head an' took his own turkey an' come on home, dat's all. (triumphantly) Yuh see y'll don't knoww whut you talkin' 'bout. Now, I done set in de court house an' heard de white folks law from mornin' till night. (He flips his Bible shut.) I done read dis book from lid tuh lid an' I knows de law. You got tuh have uh weepon tuh commit uh 'sault. An' taint in no white folks law an taint in dis Bible dat no mule bone is no weapon. I

CLARKE (after a moment of dead silence) I God, whut's dat you say?

SIMMS (sitting down and crossing his legs and folding his hands upon his Bible) You heard me. I say you ain't got no case 'ginst dis boy an' you got tuh turn him go.

SINGLETARY (jumping up) Brother Chairman—

CLARKE (raps once and nods recognition) You got de floor.

SINGLETARY I ain't book-learnt an' I ain't rubbed de hair offen my head agin no college wall, but I know when uh 'sault been committed. I says Jim Weston did 'sault Davie. (He points at Dave's head.) An' steal his turkey. Everybody knows Jim can't hunt wid Dave. An' he 'saulted Dave too.

SIMMS (arrogantly) Prove it!

(Singletary stands there silent and puzzled. The Methodist side breaks into a triumphant shout of "Oh Mary, don't you weep, don't you moan, Pharaoh's army got drownded." Singletary sinks into his seat. When they have shouted out three choruses, Simms arises to speak.)

I move dat we sing doxology and bring dis meetin' to uh close. We'se all workin' people, Brother Mayor. Dismiss us so we kin gwan back to our work. De sun is two hours high yet. (looks towards the Methodist side) I move dat we adjourn.

WALTER

I second de motion.

SINGLETARY (arising slowly) Hold on there uh minute wid dat motion. Dis ain't no lodge meetin'. Dis is uh court an' bofe sides got uh right tuh talk. (motions towards Simms' Bible) Youse uh letter learnt man but I kin read dat Bible some too. Lemme take it uh minute.

SIMMS I ain't gointer do it. Any preacher dat amounts to uh hill uh beans would have his own Bible.

CLARKE
I God, Singletary, you right here in yo' own church. Come on up here an' read out yo' pulpit Bible. I God, don't mind me being up here. Come on up.

(A great buzzing breaks out all over the church as Singletary mounts the pulpit. Clarke raps for order. Simms begins to turn the leaves of the Bible.)

SIMMS Brother Mayor, you oughter let us outa here. You ain't got no case 'ginst dis boy. Don't waste our time for nothin'. Leave us go home.

CLARKE Aw, dry up, Simms. You done talked yo' talk. I God, leave Singletary talk his. (to Singletary) Step on out when you ready, Rev.

REV. SINGLETARY (Reading) It says here in Judges 18:18 dat Samson slewed three thousand [Note: corrected missing space] Philistines wid de jawbone of an ass.

SIMMS (on his feet) Yeah, but dis wasn't no ass. Dis was uh mule, Brother Mayor. Dismiss dis meetin' and less all go home.

SINGLETARY Yeah, but he was half-ass. A ass is uh mule's daddy and he's biggern uh ass, too. (emphatic gestures) Everybody knows dat–even de lil chillun.

SIMMS (standing) Yeah, but we didn't come here to talk about no asses, neither no half asses, nor no mule daddies. (laughter from de Methodists) We come to law uh boy for 'sault an' larceny.

SINGLETARY (very patiently) We'se comin' to dat pint now. Dat's de second claw uh de sentence wese expoundin'. I say Jim Weston did have uh weepon in his hand when he 'saulted Dave. Cause y'all knows if de daddy is dangerous, den de son is dangerous too. An' y'all knows dat de further back you gits on uh mule de more dangerous he gits an' if de jawbone slewed three thousand people, by de time you gits back tuh his hocks, its pizen enough tuh kill ten thousand. Taint no gun in de world ever kilt dat many mens. Taint no knives nor no razors ever kilt no three thousand people. Now, folkses, I ast y'all whut kin be mo' dangarous dan uh mule bone? (to Clarke) Brother Mayor, Jim didn't jes' lam Dave an walk off. (very emphatic) He 'saulted him wid de deadliest weepon there is in de world an' while he was layin' unconscious, he stole his turkey an' went. Brother Mayor, he's uh criminal an' oughter be run outa dis peaceful town.

(Great chorus of approval from Baptist Clarke begins to rap for order.)

SIMMS (attending) Brother Mayor, I object. I have studied jury and I know what I'm talkin' about.

CLARKE Aw dry up, Simms. Youse entirely out of order. You may be slick, but you kin stand another greasing. Rev. Singletary is right. I God, I knows de law when I hear it. Stand up dere, Jim.

(Jim rises very slowly. Simms rises also.)

CLARKE Set down, Simms. I God, I know where to find you when I want you. (Simms sits.) Jim, I find you guilty as charged an' I wants you to git outa my town and stay gone for two years. (to Lum) Brother Marshall, you see dat he gits outa town befo' dark. An' you folks dats so anxious to fight, git on off dis church grounds befo' you start. And don't use no knives and no guns and no mule bones. Court's dismissed.

CURTAIN

ACT III

Scene I

SETTING: Curtain goes up on a stretch of railroad track with a luxurious Florida forest on the backdrop. Entrances left and right. It is near sundown.

ACTION: When the curtain goes up there is no one on the stage, but there is a tremendous noise and hub-bub off stage right. There are yells of derision, shouts of anger. Part of the mob is trying to keep Jim in town and a part is driving him off. After a full minute of this, Jim enters with his guitar hanging around his neck and his coat over his shoulder. The sun is dropping low and red thru the forest. He is looking back angrily and shouting back at the mob. A small missile is thrown after him. Jim drops his coat and guitar and grabs up a piece of brick and threatens to throw it.

JIM (Running back the way he came and hurls the brick with all his might.) I'll kill some of youole box-ankled niggers–(grabs up another piece of brick) I'm out yo' ole town–now jus' some of you ole half-pint Baptists let yo' wooden God and Cornstalk Jesus fool you to hit me! (Threatens to throw. There are some frightened screams and the mob is heard running back.) I'm glad I'm out yo' ole town, anyhow. I ain't never comin' back no more, neither. You ole ugly-rump niggers done ruint de town anyhow.

(There is complete silence off stage. Jim walks a few steps then sits down on the railroad embankment facing the audience. Jim pulls off one shoe and pours the sand out. He holds the shoe in his hand a moment and looks wistfully back down the railroad track.)

JIM Lawd, folks sho is deceitful. (He puts on the shoe and looks back down the track again.) I never woulda thought people woulda acted lak dat. (Laces up the shoe) Specially Dave Carter, much as me an' him done proaged round together goin' in swimmin' and playin' ball an' serenadin' de girls an' de white folks.

(He sits there gloomily silent for a while, then looks behind him and picks up his guitar and begins to pick a tune. It is very sad. He trails off into "You may leave an' go to Halimuhfack." When he finishes he looks back at the sun and picks up his coat also.)

I never woulda thought people woulda acted lak dat. (laces up the shoe) Specially Dave Carter, much as me an' him done proaged round together, goin' in swimmin' and playin' ball an' serenadin' de girls an' de white folks. (He sits there gloomily silent for a while then looks behind him and picks up his guitar and beings to pick a tune. It is very sad. He trails off into "You may leave and go to Halimuhfack." When he finishes he looks back at the sun and picks up his coat also.) (He looks back again towards the village.) Reckon I better git on down de road an' git somewhere, Lawd knows where. (stops suddenly in his tracks and turns back towards the village and takes a step or two.) All dat mess and stink for nothin'. Dave knows good an' well I didn't mean to hurt him much. (He takes off his cap and scratches his head thoroughly, then turns again and starts on down the road towards left. Enter Daisy left walking briskly.)

DAISY

Hello, Jim.

JIM

Hello, Daisy.

(Embarrassed silence)

DAISY

I was just coming over town to see how you come out.

JIM You don't have to go way over there to find dat out–you and Dave done got me run outa town for nothin'.

DAISY

(Putting her hand on his arm) Dey didn't run you outa town, did dey?

JIM (Shaking her hand off) Whut you reckon I'm countin' Mr. Railroad's ties for–just to find out how many ties between here and Orlando?

DAISY

(Hand on his arm again) Dey *cain't* run you off like dat!

JIM Take yo' hands off me, Daisy! How come they can't run me off wid you and Dave an'–*everybody* gainst me?

DAISY I ain't opened my moff 'gainst you, Jim. I ain't said one word–I wasn't even at de old trial. My madame wouldn't let me git off. I wuz just comin' to see 'bout you now.

JIM Aw, go 'head on. You figgered I was gone too long to talk about. You was haulin' it over to town to see Dave–dat's whut was doin'–after gittin' *me* all messed up.

DAISY

(Making as if to cry) I wasn't studying 'bout no Dave.

JIM (Hopefully) Aw, don't tell me. (Sings) Ashes to ashes, dust to dust, show me a woman that a man can trust.

(Daisy is crying now.)

JIM Whut you crying for? You know you love Dave. I'm yo' monkey-man. He always could do more wid you that I could.

DAISY

Naw, you ain't no monkey-man neither. I don't want you to leave town. I didn't want y'all to be fightin' over me, nohow.

JIM Aw, rock on down de road wid dat stuff. A two-timing cloaker like you don't keer whut come off. Me and Dave been good friends ever since we was born till you had to go flouncing yourself around.

DAISY What did I do? All I did was to come over town to see you and git a mouf-ful of gum. Next thing I now y'all is fighting and carrying on.

JIM (stands silent for a while) Did you come over there Sat'day to see me sho nuff, sugar babe?

DAISY

Everybody could see dat but you.

JIM Just like I told you, Daisy. I'll say it before yo' face and behind yo' back. I could kiss you every day–just as regular as pig-bracks.

DAISY

And I tole you I could stand it too–justa s regular as you could.

JIM

(Catching her by the arm and pulling her down with him onto the rail)
Set, down here, Daisy. Less talk some chat. You want me sho
nuff–honest to God?

DAISY (coyly) 'Member whut I told you out on de lake last summer?

JIM

Sho nuff, Daisy?

(Daisy nods smilingly.)

JIM

(Sadly) But I got to go 'way. Whut we gointer to 'bout dat?

DAISY

Where you goin', Jim?

JIM

(Looking sadly down the track) God knows.

(Off stage from the same direction from which Jim entered comes the sound of whistling and tramping of feet on the ties.)

JIM (Brightening) Dat's Dave! (Frowning suspiciously) Wonder whut he doin' walking dis track? (Looks accusingly at Daisy) I bet he's goin' to yo' work-place.

DAISY

Whut for?

JIM He ain't goin' to see de madame–must be goin' to see you. (He starts to rise petulantly as Dave comes upon the scene. Daisy rises also.)

DAVE (Looks accusingly from one to the other) Whut y'all jumpin' up for? I .

JIM Whut you got to do wid us business? Tain't none of yo' business if we stand up, set down or fly like a skeeter hawk.

DAVE Who said I keered? Dis railroad belongs to de *man*–I kin walk it good as you, can't I?

JIM (Laughing exultantly) Oh yeah, Mr. Do-Dirty! You figgered you had done run me on off so you could git Daisy all by yo'self. You was headin' right for her work-place.

DAVE

I wasn't no such a thing.

JIM You was. Didn't I lear you coming down de track all whistling and everything?

DAVE

Youse a big old Georgy-something-ain't-so! I done got my belly full of
Daisy Sat'day night. She can't snore in my ear no more.

DAISY (Indignantly) Whut you come here low-rating me for, Dave Carter? I ain't done nothin' to you but treat you white. Who come rubbed yo' ole head for you yestiddy if it wasn't me?

DAVE Yeah, you rubbed my head all right, and I lakted dat. But everybody say you done toted a pan to Joe Clark's barn for Jim before I seen you.

DAISY Think I was going to let Jim there thout nothing fitten for a dog to eat?

DAVE That's all right, Daisy. If you want to pay Jim for r knockin' me in de head, all right. But I'm a man in a class–in a class to myself and nobody knows my name.

JIM (Snatching Daisy around to face him) Was you over to Dave's house yestiddy rubbing his ole head and cloaking wid him to run me outa town–and me locked up in dat barn wid de cows and mules?

DAISY (Sobbing) All both of y'all hollerin' at me an' fussin' me just cause I tries to be nice–and neither one of y'all don't keer nothin' bout me.

(Both boys glare at each other over Daisy's head and both try to hug her at the same time. She violently wrenches herself away from both and makes as if to move on.)

Leave me go! Take yo' rusty pams offen me. I'm going on back to my work-place. I just got off to see bout y'all and look how y'all treat me.

JIM Wait a minute, Daisy. I love you like God loves Gabriel–and dat's His best angel.

DAVE Daisy, I love you harder than detthunder can bump a stump–if I don't–God's a gopher.

DAISY
(Brightening) Dat's de first time you ever said so.

DAVE and JIM
Who?

JIM
Whut you hollering "who" for? Yo' foot don't fit no limb.

DAVE Speak when you spoken to–come when you called, next fall you'll be my coon houn' dog.

JIM Table dat discussion. (Turning to Daisy) You ain't never give me no chance to talk wid you right.

DAVE You made *me* feel like you was trying to put de Ned book on me all de time. Do you love me sho nuff, Daisy?

DAISY (Blooming again into coquetry) Aw, y'all better stop dat. You know you don't mean it.

DAVE
Who don't mean it? Lemme tell you something, mama, if you was mine I wouldn't have you counting no ties wid yo' pretty lil toes. Know whut I'd do?

DAISY
(Coyly) Naw, whut would you do?

DAVE
I'd buy a whole passenger train and hire some mens to run it for you.

DAISY
(Happily) Oo-ooh, Dave.

JIM (to Dave)
   De wind may blow, de door may slam
Dat whut you shootin' ain't worth a dam.

(to Daisy) I'd buy you a great big ole ship–and then baby, I'd buy you a ocean to[Note: corrected missing space] sail yo' ship on.

DAISY

(Happily) Oo-ooh, Jim.

DAVE (to Jim)

A long train, a short caboose

Dat lie whut you shootin', ain't no use.

(to Daisy) Miss Daisy, know what I'd do for you?

DAISY

Naw, whut?

DAVE

I'd like uh job cleanin out de Atlantic Ocean jus for you.

DAISY

Don't fool me now, papa.

DAVE I couldn't fool *you*, Daisy, cause anything I say bout lovin' you, I don't keer how big it is, it wouldn't be half de truth. Y

DAVE

I'd come down de river riding a mud cat and leading a minnow.

DAISY

Lawd, Dave, you sho is propaganda.

JIM (Peevishly) Naw he ain't–he's just lying–he's a noble liar. Know whut I'd do if you was mine?

DAISY

Naw, Jim.

JIM

I'd make a panther wash yo' dishes and a 'gator chop yo' wood for you.

DAVE Daisy, how come you [Note: corrected missing space] let Jim lie lak dat? He's as big a liar as he is a [Note: corrected missing space] man. But sho nuff now, laying all sides to jokes, Jim, there don't even know how to answer you. If you don't b'lieve it, ast him something.

DAISY (to Jim) You like me much, Jim?

JIM

(Enthusiastically) Yeah, Daisy, I sho do.

DAVE (Triumphant) See dat! I tole you he didn't know how to answer nobocy like you. If he was talking to some of them ol' funny looking gals over town he'd be answering 'em just right. But he got to learn how to answer *you*. Now you ast *me* something and see how I answer you.

DAISY

Do you like me, Dave?

DAVE (Very properly in a falsetto voice) Yes ma'am! Dat's de way to answer swell folks like you. Furthermore, less we prove which one [Note: corrected missing space] of us love you de best right now. (To Jim) Jim, how much time owuld you do on de chain-gang for dis 'oman?

JIM

Twenty years and like it.

DAVE See dat, Daisy? Dat nigger ain't willing to do no time for you. I'd *beg* de judge to gimme life. (Both Jim and Dave laugh)

DAISY Y'all doin' all dis bookooing out here on de railroad track but I bet y'all crazy 'bout Bootsie and Teets and a whole heap of others.

JIM Cross my feet and hope to die! I'd ruther see all de other wimmenfolks in de world dead than for[Note: corrected missing space] you to have de tooth-ache.

DAVE If I was dead any any other woman come near my coffin de undertaker would have to do his job all over–cause I'd git right up and walk off. Furthermore, Miss Daisy, ma'am, also m'am, which would *you* ruther be a lark a flying or a dove a settin'–ma'am also ma'am?

DAISY
'Course I'd ruther be a dove.

JIM
Miss Daisy, ma'am, also ma'am–if you marry dis nigger over my head, I'm going to git me a green hickory club and season it over yo' head.

DAVE
Don't you be skeered, baby–papa kin take keer a *you*. (to Jim) Counting from de finger (suiting the action to the word) back to the thumb–start anything I got you some.

JIM
Aw, I don't want no more fight wid you, Dave.

DAVE Who said anything about fighting? We just provin' who love Daisy de best. (to Daisy) Now, which one of us you think love you de best?

DAISY
Deed I don't know, Dave.

DAVE
Baby, I'd walk de water for you–and tote a mountain on my head while I'm walkin'.

JIM Know whut I'd do, honey babe? If you was a thousand miles from home and you didn't have no ready-made money and you had to walk all de way, walkin' till yo' feet start to rolling, just like a wheel, and I was riding way up in de sky, I'd step backwards offa dat airyplane just to walk home wid you.

DAISY (Falling on Jim's neck) Jim, when you talk to me like dat I just can't stand it. Less us git married right now.

JIM
Now you talkin' like a blue-back speller. Less go!

DAVE
(Sadly) You gointer leave me lak dis, Daisy?

DAISY (Sadly) I likes you, too, Dave, I sho do. But I can't marry both of y'all at de same time.

JIM
Aw, come on, Daisy–sun's gettin' low. (He starts off pulling Daisy.)

DAVE
Whut's I'm gointer do? (Walking after them)

JIM Gwan back and hunt turkeys–you make out you so touchous nobody can't tell you yo' eye is black thout you got to run git de law.

DAVE

(Almost tearfully) Aw Jim, shucks! Where y'all going?

(Daisy comes to an abrupt halt and stops Jim)

DAISY

That's right, Honey. Where *is* we goin' sho nuff?

JIM (Sadly) Deed I don't know, baby. They just sentenced [Note: corrected missing space] me to go–they didn't say where and I don't know.

DAISY How we goin' know how to go when [Note: corrected missing space] we don't know where we goin'?

(Jim looks at Dave as if he expects some help but Dave stands sadly silent. Jim takes a few steps forward as if to go on. Daisy makes a step or two, unwillingly, then looks behind her and stops. Dave looks as if he will follow them.)

DAISY Jim! (He stops and turns) Wait a minute! Whut we gointer do when we git there?

JIM

Where?

DAISY

Where we goin'?

JIM

I done tole you I don't know where it is.

DAISY

But how we gointer git something to eat and a place to stay?

JIM

Play my box for de white folks and dance just like I been doing.

DAISY

You can't take keer of me on dat, not where we hafta pay rent.

JIM (Looks appealingly at Dave, then away quickly) Well, I can't help *dat*, can I?

DAISY (Brightly) I tell you whut, Jim! Less us don't go nowhere. They sentenced you to leave Eatonville and youse almost a mile from de city limits already. Youse in Maitland now. Supposin' you come live on de white folks' place wid me after we git married. Eatonville ain't got nothin' to do wid you livin' in Maitland.

JIM

Dat's a good idea, Daisy.

DAISY (Jumping into his arms) And lissen, honey, you don't have to be beholden to nobody. You can throw dat ole box away if you want to. I know where you can get a *swell* job.

JIM

(Sheepishly) Doin' whut? (Looks lovingly at his guitar)

DAISY (Almost dancing) Yard man. All you have to do is wash windows, and sweep de sidewalk, and scrub off de steps and porch and hoe up de weeds and rake up de leaves and dig a few holes now and then with a spade–to plant some trees and things like that. It's a good steady job.

JIM (After a long deliberation) You see, Daisy, de mayor and corporation told me to go on off and I oughter go.

DAISY

Well, I'm not going tippin' down no railroad track like a Maltese cat.
I wasn't brought up knockin' round from here to yonder.

JIM Well, I wasn't brought up wid no spade in my hand–and ain't going to start it now.

DAISY But sweetheart, we got to live, ain't we? We got to git hold of money before we kin do anything. I don't mean to stay in de white folks' kitchen all my days.

JIM Yeah, all dat's true, but you couldn't buy a flea a waltzing jacket wid de money *I'm* going to make wid a hoe and spade.

DAISY

(Getting tearful) You don't want me. You don't love me.

JIM Yes, I do, darling, I love you. Youse de one letting a spade come between us. (He caresses her.) I loves you and you only. You don't see *me* dragging a whole gang of farming tools into us business, do you?

DAISY (stiffly) Well, I ain't going to marry no man that ain't going to work and take care of me.

JIM I don't mind working if de job ain't too heavy for me. I ain't going to bother wid nothin' in my hands heavier than dis box–and I totes it round my neck 'most of de time. I kin go out and hunt you some game when times gits tight.

DAISY Don't strain yo'self huntin' nothin' for me. I ain't goin' to eat nobody's settin' hen. (She turns to DAVE finally.)

JIM

Whut ole sittin hen? Ain't you and Lum done et up de turkey
I–I–bought?

DAISY You might of brought it, but Dave sho kilt it. You couldn't hit de side of uh barn wid uh bass fiddle.

DAVE

Course I kilt it, and I kilt it for you, but I didn't kill none for
Lum Boger. De clean head hound!

(Daisy turns to Dave finally)

DAISY Well, I reckon you loves me the best anyhow. You wouldn't talk to me like Jim did, would you, Dave?

DAVE

Naw, I wouldn't say whut he said a-tall.

DAISY

(Cuddling up to him) Whut would *you* say, honey?

DAVE I'd say dat box was too heavy for me to fool wid. I wouldn't tote nothing my gun and my hat and I feel like I'm 'busing myself sometie totin' dat.

DAISY

(Outraged) Don't you mean to work none?

DAVE

Wouldn't hit a lick at a snake.

DAISY I don't blame *you*, Dave (looks down at his feet) cause toting dem feet of yourn is enough to break down your constitution.

DAVE They carries me wherever I wants to go. Daisy, you marry Jim cause I don't want to come between y'all. He's my buddy.

JIM Come to think of it, Dave, she was yourn first. You take and handle dat spade for her.

DAVE You heard her say it is all I can do to lift up dese feets and put 'em down. Where I'm going to git any time to wrassle wid any hoes and shovels? You kin git round better'n me. You done won Daisy–I give in. I ain't going to bite no friend of mine in de back.

DAISY Both of you niggers can git yo' hat en' yo' heads an' git on down de road. Neither one of y'all don't have to have me. I got a good job and plenty men begging for yo' chance.

JIM Dat's right, Daisy, you go git you one them mens whut don't mind smelling mules–and beating de white folks to de barn every morning. I don't wanta be bothered wid nothin' but dis box.

DAVE And I can't strain wid nothin' but my feets and my gun. I kin git mo' turkey gobblers, but never no job.

(Daisy walks slowly away in the direction from which she came. Both watch her a little wistfully for a minute. The sun is setting.)

DAVE

Guess I better be gitin' on back–it's most dark. Where you goin, Jim?

JIM

I don't know, Dave. Down de road, I reckon.

DAVE

Whyncher come on back to town? Taint no use you proagin' up and down de railroad track when you got a home.

JIM

They done lawed me way from it for hittin' you wid dat bone.

DAVE Dat ain't nothin'. It was my head you hit. An' if I don't keer whut dem ole ugly-rump niggers got to do wid it?

JIM

They might not let me come in town.

DAVE (Seizing Jim's arm and facing him back toward the town.) They better! Look here, Jim, if they try to keep you out dat town we'll go out to dat swamp and git us a mule bone a piece and come back and boil dat stew down to a low gravy.

JIM

You mean dat Dave? (Dave nods his head eagerly.)

DAVE Us wasn't mad wid one 'nother nohow. Come on less go back to town. Dem mullet heads better leave me be, too. (Picks up a heavy stick) I wish Lum would come tellin' me bout de law when I got all dis law in *my* hands. An' de rest of dem 'gator-face jigs–if they ain't got a whole set of mule bones and a good determination they better not bring de mess up.

CURTAIN

Manufactured By: RR Donnelley
                     Breinigsville, PA USA
                     July, 2010